A MEMOIR
OF THE
MISSILE AGE

A MEMOIR

OF THE

MISSILE AGE

One Man's Journey

Vitaly Leonidovich Katayev

Project Advisor,
Ksenia Kostrova

HOOVER INSTITUTION PRESS

STANFORD UNIVERSITY   STANFORD, CALIFORNIA

The Hoover Institution on War, Revolution and Peace, founded at Stanford University in 1919 by Herbert Hoover, who went on to become the thirty-first president of the United States, is an interdisciplinary research center for advanced study on domestic and international affairs. The views expressed in its publications are entirely those of the authors and do not necessarily reflect the views of the staff, officers, or Board of Overseers of the Hoover Institution.

www.hoover.org

Hoover Institution Press Publication No. 622

Hoover Institution at Leland Stanford Junior University,
Stanford, California 94305-6003

First printing 2015
20   19   18   17   16   15   7   6   5   4   3   2   1

Manufactured in the United States of America

The paper used in this publication meets the minimum Requirements of the American National Standard for Information Sciences—Permanence of Paper for Printed Library Materials, ANSI/NISO Z39.48-1992. ♾

Cataloging-in-Publication Data is available from the Library of Congress.

ISBN: 978-0-8179-1474-5 (cloth. : alk. paper)
ISBN: 978-0-8179-1475-2 (pbk. : alk. paper)
ISBN: 978-0-8179-1476-9 (epub)
ISBN: 978-0-8179-1477-6 (mobi)
ISBN: 978-0-8179-1478-3 (PDF)

A note to readers

Vitaly Katayev died in 2001. He wrote his memoir before his death. This book is based on Katayev's original manuscript, materials from his personal archive, and fragments of his interview for the oral history project of the Moscow State Institute of International Relations and the Hoover Institution at Stanford University. This material was prepared for publication by his granddaughter Ksenia Kostrova.

Portions of this memoir were translated from Russian to English by Natalia Alexandrova and Irina Makarova. Additional excerpts were translated by Roman Ozornov and edited by Scott Bean of the Russian Translation Company.

Katayev's papers are deposited at the Hoover Institution Library and Archives.

Contents

Foreword

The most remarkable thing about Vitaly Katayev, my grandfather, is that he witnessed the dawn of the age of nuclear-armed missiles, as a designer, and then became deeply involved in disarmament in the late 1980s and early 1990s. This was a real journey, a willing transformation of mind.

As a designer, my grandfather knew not only the long, hard labor that went into building nuclear weapons but also their danger. No one can really appreciate what it meant for one of the "parents" of a weapon to eliminate it. But he believed in this way and thought it was best for the world, no matter how hard it might be.

The main challenge in disarmament was to overcome the resistance of the military. My grandfather felt that members of the military were the most conservative people imaginable. But still, he and his colleagues pushed successfully to scale back the arsenals and eliminate the weapons.

In 1992, my grandfather was deeply disappointed by the new Yeltsin administration. He pointed out that new, inexperienced defense officials removed the old experts only because they were Communist Party members and part of some "old school." He said the disarmament process could have been easier and faster without this unreasonable ejection of people who had put their lives into making the world safer and who understood the process in every detail. He could not stand the situation and decided to quit.

Overall, the process of creating nuclear weapons as well as disarmament was a political one. A truly great specialist must combine sensitivity to the political demands of the leadership with an acute understanding of the technology. My grandfather was an expert of this kind. He had the final say when it came to the technical details in disarmament treaties. Leaders would often sign the memos he prepared without even reading them. And he took upon himself responsibility for the technical information included in the treaties.

I think the reason my grandfather deposited his archive at the Hoover Institution was his belief that his notes and documents should be available to everyone and would help to deepen our understanding of the nuclear age.

Ksenia Kostrova
Moscow
November 2014

Preface

The idea of writing a memoir nagged at me for a long while. I hesitated because time seemed short, and I wasn't certain that the topic of rocket technology and military policy would interest a broad circle of people. However, after giving several long interviews and taking part in television programs devoted to the period of the Cold War, I realized that this information can be interesting and that there is an audience.

Almost all my life I worked in the military-industrial complex of the Soviet Union, studying it from the inside out. Not only did I observe the unfolding of the Cold War, but I also participated in the process. I am a specialist in aviation and rocket systems and started by working for design bureaus. I rose to leading designer of a number of ground-based strategic rocket systems built at one of the world's biggest rocket centers, in Ukraine, at Yuzhnoye Design Bureau in the city of Dnepropetrovsk, where 70 percent of the Soviet ground-based strategic rockets were built. There, I designed the fuel system for heavy-rocket booster RK-100 (an alternative variant of the booster for the moon program).[1] I went to the Baikonur test range where I prepared the next launch of an R-16 after one of these rockets exploded, killing many military men and civilian specialists. The commander-in-chief of the Strategic Rocket Forces, Marshal Mitrofan Nedelin, was among them. My next rocket for a short period of time was a well-known heavy missile, the R-36, a prototype of SS-18. Then I worked on the Interkosmos system. This system of international cooperation on rocket technology, because of the conditions of secrecy, was making slow progress. At the beginning, we used the space booster from the R-12 rocket and satellites made in Dnepropetrovsk. Then I handed Interkosmos over to leading designer Leonid Kuchma (who later became president of Ukraine) and took up the mobile, railroad-based strategic rocket complex RT-23. The last missile complex on which I worked as leading designer in the Yuzhnoye Design Bureau was the SS-18.

During this time, I had to visit Moscow four or five times a month. There was a special charter plane, hired by our bureau, which flew from Dnepropetrovsk to Moscow twice a week. In Moscow, I would lobby the rocket-complex project in the so-called "Bermuda triangle"—the Central Committee, the Council of Ministers, and the Ministry of Defense. I also had to visit plants and contractors.

At the end of 1974, despite my strong resistance, I was transferred to Moscow to work at the Communist Party's Central Committee Defense Industry Department (it was later renamed the Defense Department of the Central Committee, which I shall use here). I worked as instructor, then as head of a sector, and later as deputy head, supervising the development and construction of the most modern strategic sea-based systems: the R-31, R-29R, R-39 (on the famous Typhoon submarine, which displaced 42,000 tons of water), and the R-29RM.[2] Simultaneously, I had to deal with issues of Soviet military policy, as well as the limitation and reduction of weapons.

While in Dnepropetrovsk and Moscow, I closely collaborated with the academician chief designers Mikhail Yangel and Viktor Makeyev.[3] The public at large knew nothing about them, but they designed some of the most significant ground- and sea-based combat rocket systems.

My approach to everything was based on systems. In the 1980s, I participated in organizing a system of working out initiatives and proposals on military and military-technical problems called the interdepartmental working group. I participated directly in that process, including international negotiations, helping to work out security concepts and write treaty texts. It was very intensive work. Suffice it to say that within a year I had to process about two thousand secret or ciphered telegrams from all foreign services. In 1989, I received 80.3 percent of all telegrams of the Defense Department.

With the introduction of presidential rule in the Gorbachev years, the Defense Department was taken out of the Central Committee because it was not part of the party structure. It was transformed into a department for defense and security under the president of the Soviet Union. I was its last head. After Gorbachev left, I had to disband it. Some of the elite specialists of the department were transferred into the service of state advisors of the Russian Federation on defense conversion.

Other highlights of my career include working as a professor at the Moscow Aviation Institute in the department of systems analysis and working with centers for nonproliferation in Moscow, Washington, and Monterey, California, and with universities abroad: Stanford University (Hoover Institution and Morrison Institute), Oxford University, and Ohio State University (Mershon Center).

Throughout my career, I maintained scientific and technical links with the Russian aviation institutes and rocket design organizations. In the first part of the book, I offer snapshots from my time connected to this industry in Omsk, Dnepropetrovsk, Baikonur, and Miass. Working for the Defense Department, I oversaw matters of sea-based strategic missiles, dealt with military policy, including the limitation and reduction of weapons, and participated in international negotiations. In the second part of the book, I offer this insider's view, from Moscow, of Soviet arms development and control.

Introduction

David E. Hoffman

Vitaly Leonidovich Katayev was an eyewitness to history. He saw the arms race accelerating at an absurd and inexplicable pace, and he understood why. His perspective was from inside the Soviet system, in an office that was devoted to analysis of arms control and defense matters in the Central Committee of the Soviet Communist Party and later in an interdepartmental working group. Mr. Katayev was a skilled designer and an acute observer. His recollections in this book, along with documents he deposited at the Hoover Institution Library and Archives, offer an extraordinary window into Soviet decisions and calculations.

When President Ronald Reagan first met General Secretary Mikhail Gorbachev in Geneva in 1985, he said, "Nations do not mistrust each other because of arms, but they arm each other because of mistrust." It was an old speech line for Reagan, but it rang true. The greatest dangers of the Cold War came not from the weapons but from the mindset of the people who created and operated them. Seeing each other through a veil of suspicion, the superpowers often wrongly judged each other's intentions and actions. There were missile gaps, bomber gaps, deliberate deceptions, and impenetrable walls of secrecy. The importance of Mr. Katayev's memoir and the document collection is that they shed light on these dark corners of the arms race from the Soviet side, which is in many ways the least understood.

In 1990 and 1991, the United States Department of Defense commissioned an unusual study. The goal was to send a qualified expert to the Soviet Union at a time when it was opening up—but before the collapse—and interview top officials about strategic thinking and military policy. The senior author of the study was John G. Hines, and he carried out a wide range of fascinating interviews with generals, policy makers, and party officials. The study was titled "Soviet Intentions, 1965–1985" and was completed in September 1995.[1] One of the most important conclusions of this study was that the West had misunderstood how the Soviet Union made decisions in the years of the nuclear arms race. The West failed to realize that it was the Soviet military-industrial complex which held the upper hand, not the military services, in deciding what to build and what the strategy would be. The defense establishment—the design bureaus, factories, and associated ministries—prospered and expanded during the years of Soviet leader Leonid Brezhnev, who had come out of the missile industry. Mr. Katayev helped Mr. Hines with the study; he was deeply knowledgeable about the workings of this military-industrial complex. He had worked in the missile design bureaus and then in the decision-making machinery in Moscow.

In the Soviet Union, the military-industrial complex was not just a concept but a real set of institutions that were guided by a formal Military-Industrial Commission. The defense-industry establishment drove the growth of Soviet military expansion, not the uniformed military, as the United States and Western nations had assumed. Thus, Mr. Katayev's life and times, indeed his entire career, are a journey through this most important and often-overlooked archipelago of launching pads, design bureaus, factories, and policy-making offices.

The years of the Cold War left many in the West with a sense that the Soviet Union was highly regimented. But Mr. Katayev's memoir portrays a system that also thrived on improvisation and included some competition, as well as sizeable overlap and overkill. For example, he tells the story of how the boss of the Omsk Civil Aviation Plant, where Mr. Katayev was working early in his career, sought to bid for a job building a new kind of airplane by bluffing—he claimed that assembly racks were already prepared at his plant and they could begin work on the plane the next day, when in fact none existed on the factory floor. When a commission decided to fly to Omsk to check, the boss ordered an all-night effort to prepare them, a job that usually took one or two months. Overnight, Mr. Katayev writes, "a Potemkin village was built in the assembly workshop." The factory got the job.

In this memoir, Mr. Katayev captures the drama of the Soviet system when it first raced forward and was then hauled into reverse as Mr. Gorbachev came to power and began the process of negotiating arms control agreements with Mr. Reagan. Mr. Katayev enjoyed a ring-side seat when some of the most sensitive decisions about arms control were being made, in particular about whether Moscow should make concessions on nuclear-weapons delivery systems. Mr. Katayev recalls the chief of the General Staff of the Armed Forces, Marshal Sergei Akhromeyev, agonizing over proposed missile cutbacks and at one point turning to Mr. Katayev in a soft voice and saying, "If this really happens, I'll hand in my party card." Marshal Akhromeyev later became a leading advisor to Mr. Gorbachev in the arms race in reverse that followed.

Mr. Katayev, precise and careful, loved lists and charts. He filled notebooks with them, in neat handwriting, often accompanied by drawings. These notebooks and the entire document collection, while complex, offer a deeper understanding of Soviet decision-making and record some highly technical aspects of the arms race that have not previously been known. For example, Mr. Katayev's charts of Soviet flight tests show that the largest missiles, such as the SS-18, were not as accurate as the United States intelligence estimates had suggested. This is important because it suggests that American fears about Soviet missile capabilities were exaggerated. Those fears were great and had prompted Mr. Reagan to warn that the United States faced a "window of vulnerability" to Soviet missile attack in the 1980s. In fact, as Mr. Katayev's records show, that window didn't really exist.

Perhaps most importantly, Mr. Katayev's memoir and documents will help Americans see the depths and dangers of suspicion and miscalculation during the Cold War. Mr. Katayev wrote a
monograph at one point about Soviet perceptions of Mr. Reagan's
Strategic Defense Initiative, his dream of a globe-spanning missile
defense system. The monograph, which is included in the Hoover
collection, reflects the enormous confusion that welled up among
Soviet analysts. They had been told by the best Soviet physicists that
Mr. Reagan's plan for a missile that could shoot down a missile was
technically not possible before the end of the century. "What is it
being done for?" the Soviet specialists asked themselves, according
to Mr. Katayev; "In the name of what, are the Americans, famous
for their pragmatism, opening their wallet for the most grandiose
project in the history of the United States when the technical and
economic risks of a crash exceed all thinkable limits?" He writes
that some Soviet officials began to suspect that Mr. Reagan's plan
was a "Hollywood village of veneer and cardboard." And a few
Soviet experts held an even darker view of Mr. Reagan's goals. They
concluded that the Americans were always distinguished by their
systematic approach to problems, that they "do nothing in vain."
Rather than a hoax or bluff, they decided the Strategic Defense Initiative was a cover story for a gigantic hidden effort to subsidize
American defense contractors, save them from "bankruptcy," and
produce a fresh surge of superior military high technology. Perhaps,
Mr. Katayev writes, this "was the major underwater part of the SDI
iceberg."

Mr. Katayev's monograph shows how Soviet leaders were often
hobbled by a poor understanding of what was happening in the
United States, but his materials also demonstrate that Americans,
too, had a weak grasp of what was happening in Moscow, before
and after Mr. Gorbachev came to power. Many U.S. analysts could
not see signs of change in 1985 when Mr. Gorbachev became general
secretary. But Mr. Katayev's documents show that when the designers
and defense plants pressed Gorbachev that year to build a massive
Soviet response to Reagan's missile defense system, Gorbachev did

not go along. He did not want an arms race in space, nor on the ground, and was preparing for a radical new direction. The misunderstandings on both sides were a symptom of the deepest chasm of the Cold War. Each side remained a black box to the other. In this memoir, and in Mr. Katayev's papers, we have a valuable key with which to open the Soviet black box.

PART I

SNAPSHOTS FROM A CAREER IN SOVIET ROCKET DESIGN

I am going to start my story from the moment of graduating from the Kazan Aviation Institute, when I did not yet suspect where my life would take me. Here are snapshots from what turned out to be a career in Soviet rocket design.

CHAPTER 1

Omsk Civil Aviation Plant

After finishing at the Kazan Aviation Institute (KAI) in 1956, I wanted to get assigned to a job in Dnepropetrovsk. But that year the placing commission did not get any requests from the Dnepropetrovsk Design Bureau for graduates of KAI.[1] Besides, my ranking based on the sum of all my marks, as specified in the diploma index, was thirty-third out of one hundred graduates. So to be sure, a place in sunny Ukraine was not likely to be mine anyway. Gerold Petrov, fellow Kazan graduate and an old friend from the aviation modeling club in Perm, where I had spent my childhood and youth, would get employment first, as the top student.

When Gerold cheerfully emerged from the doors of the commission, everybody surrounded him. "What were they offering? Which cities? Where will they send you?" We peppered him with questions. We were anxious: practically our entire futures would be decided in the next few minutes.

"They asked me where I would like to go," Gerold reported. "I replied Gorky. They said, 'Good, you'll go to Gorky.' That's all. I don't know what other places are available."[2]

At last Gerold's eyes found me and he came over.

"Are you still aiming at Ukraine?" he asked. "Listen, let's go to Gorky together."

"All right. If there's no place in Ukraine, I'll ask for Gorky," I replied.

My turn came. I was nervous like never before. Will my dream of Ukraine come true? Why Ukraine? What made it attractive to a Russian guy from the Urals? My life's goal had been to go there ever since my early years in Perm. I had read technical journals there and had contemplated my future while chopping whole piles of firewood for the fireplace in our tiny log house with ice-glazed windows.

My father had carefully pushed me towards making a plan for what would happen after the institute.

"Where have you decided to go after the institute, to our place here, or elsewhere?" he inquired.

"As they decide."

"And what have *you* decided?"

I didn't have a ready answer. I hadn't decided. I was comfortable floating along. And when I did think about it? Number one: interesting work, a designer's job would be best of all. I had been a designer since early childhood. I had made models of ships. Then I had become an aviation model maker, a champion of the Perm region. The Perm newspaper had twice mentioned me with a flattering forecast for my future. The father of my comrade Vovka Medvedev had told me many times, as he checked my handmade models built out of leftover aviation scrap, "Vitaly, you will make an excellent technologist. Go work at the factory; they need guys like you there." Mr. Medvedev was a factory worker, yacht sailor, and biker who did everything with his own hands. Hence, I thought to myself, "I ought to work in a factory, an aviation one, of course. I ought to choose a city that has moderate seasons, not too northern yet not too southern, and not too far from the seashore." I had a girlfriend in Perm in student days: Allochka Sklyarevskaya. I made my plans known to her first. She liked them. This inspired me, too.

At the institute in Kazan, an aviation industry journal had come my way. The journal was considered secret. One article described some fantastic technology: a specialist from the Dnepropetrovsk factory was suggesting manufacturing the shell of a small air-to-surface rocket out of cement reinforced with metal net. But there was a little bit more information in the article than just a description of the technology. "Good, they deal with rockets at that plant. This is a serious business, I must pay attention," I had decided. I had started looking for any information about the Dnepropetrovsk plant in technical journals. Very occasionally, articles had slipped in: about the automatic welding of pipelines, or about pressing, or about composite materials. Seeing my interest, my friends had helped me find some of these articles. Later, I learnt that there were job assignments to this factory and its design bureau from our institute. By the end of my studies, I had a clear image of my goal: Dnepropetrovsk.

And so, on "judgment day," I stood in front of the institute committee for job assignments. I was so nervous I didn't even notice who the committee members were.

"So, what are you going to say? Any desires?" they demanded.

"Dnepropetrovsk!"

"Hmm. We have no requests from Dnepropetrovsk this year."

"Gorky then."

"All vacancies for Gorky are already distributed. We wanted to offer you the opportunity to stay in Kazan. What's your opinion?"

I was prepared for this offer. I had written a rather interesting thesis at the institute and had given an original presentation. Many people had come to hear me defend it. While I talked, I saw the secretary of the thesis committee show some pages to its members, and they smiled their approval. When announcing the marks, the chairman of the thesis committee modulated his voice in some particularly approving way regarding my five mark and said that the research for the thesis should be reported one more time at a special conference.[3] I had thought at that point: they are going to offer me a position in Kazan. And so they did.

"My opinion is negative," I replied. "I'd rather go to Omsk."

"Oh. Very good!"

The Omsk Civil Aviation Plant had requested twenty-five graduates that year. The plant was planning to join the race for getting a sought-after state order—building the first passenger jet plane, the Tu-104. But until then, none of the graduates who passed through the committee had wished to go there. For some reason, this site was considered a place of banishment for graduates with low grades. And here was a volunteer! I had been in Omsk for research before the thesis was finished. Later, when I tried to think through how my ideas could be realized, it appeared that the Omsk plant would suit me.

I arrived in Omsk in April 1956. They put me up in a group residence. Eight people were in my room, all workers except for me. One of the guys—a welder—had his mother living with him there, too; they made a makeshift bed out of chairs for her at night. They received me at the room in the group house with caution: one engineer among the workers. How is he going to act? I noticed their reticence at once. I had to think over both my behavior and topics of conversation. I tried to fit in with the life of both the room and the whole house as an equal. The other residents quickly approved: he is our kind of guy.

To me, "our kind of guy" is high praise. I got this kind of endorsement another time, years later, when I took part in preparations for my daughter's graduation party at her Moscow school. I spent a lot of time driving around Moscow with the boys: we bought food and flowers; I carried boxes and furniture with them, and I drove people places without saying "no." The kids knew: this fellow behind the wheel works at the Central Committee; he is a superimportant boss.

After the graduation party, my daughter asked, "Do you know what our boys said about you?"

"What? Cursed me for poor help?"

"Quite the contrary, they gave you a high grade, they said, 'This is our kind of guy!'"

I had asked for a job at the factory's design bureau. There, they had documentation for an Ilyushin Il-18 aircraft prototype, for which production had been terminated. They gave me blueprints of the landing gear and said, "Study!" At this point, I developed an obsessive complex. I was embarrassed by my overly simple job. I scraped old blueprints on tracing paper with a razor, made some primitive changes, got my nearest bosses to sign them, and that was it! People passed by and stared. A huge fellow sits and scrapes. This fellow should be doing a real job, yet he scrapes with a blunt razor here. This is a job to give to an uneducated schoolgirl, not to a real man.

This is what went through my mind, as I bent over old tracing paper, ashamed to look people in the eye.

But at the same time I discovered the *Znaniye* society in Omsk.[4] Earlier, I had been asked, through KAI, to give several lectures on the subject of modern aviation. Somebody had liked it, so I had given this lecture in Kazan over twenty times. I had collected many illustrations for the lectures, personally copied from magazines, and I had brought all this to Omsk with me. Through the Znaniye society, I had opportunities to deliver the lecture again in Omsk. After lecturing at the Omsk Civil Aviation Plant and other sites around Omsk, the head of the plant's information department came to me with a proposition.

"I heard you speak," he said. "You are not bad at it. Would you like to try teaching aviation disciplines at the aviation technical school, say, aerodynamics, aeromechanics, design, assembly and testing of aircraft? All this will be in the evening after working hours."

I gave this a try and ended up teaching a number of subjects until my departure from Omsk. Work at the design bureau finished at 5:30 p.m.; lectures started next door at 5:40 p.m. and ran till late at night. After lecturing, I prepared the next day's class at home till 2:00 a.m. After that came work on students' research papers and theses. This was my routine almost every day.

In my first year of work at the plant, a Council of Young Specialists —among the first in the country—was formed, and I acted as its chairman until the end of my job there.[5] Apart from upgrading the qualifications of young specialists and protecting their rights, the council was authorized to distribute housing to them. During the period of my chairmanship, we distributed eighty-six flats. Receiving housing was a strong incentive for young specialists to improve their work, but only my colleagues knew what it cost me, the chairman. "Vitaly, you have a strong nervous system," they would tell me as I sat in a big audience hall after yet another young woman specialist would have left, having failed to speed up the process of getting a flat with her loud hysterics.

The second half of the 1950s was a difficult time for the plant. The production of the front bomber Il-28—the main bomber of the

Soviet air force—was discontinued. There was quiet. The plant's director, Boris Yelenevich, spent time in Moscow trying to obtain an important contract to manufacture the Tu-104, the first passenger jet plane in regular service in the world. The contract was also interesting for the fact that the first passenger jet plane was being created on the basis of a jet bomber, the Tu-16. A large share of the testing for passenger characteristics of the plane was to be allocated to a serial-production plant. Among numerous other contenders for getting the contract was the Voronezh Aviation Plant.

Yelenevich was a jolly, lordly boss, full of importance. He liked a weighty conversation, smoked an aromatic pipe, and dressed in soft, fluffy sweaters. Usually, I would show up to see him in the evening, about the matters of the Council of Young Specialists.

"What are you going to tell me, Chairman?" Yelenevich might inquire.

"You see, this is not working too well, . . ." I might respond.

And I would start a detailed accounting of what else could be done to raise the qualification of young specialists. There were business trips here, trips to exhibitions, "know-how" competitions, requests for housing, requests for funds for youth parties, and lots of other issues about which there were disagreements with the director for personnel. Yelenevich rarely argued; on the contrary, he added his suggestions. He made lots of promises, but he didn't always fulfill them. I once reproached him about this before a plant conference of young specialists.

"Give me the list of what I'm guilty of. I'll apologize to the young people," he quickly responded.

He did apologize and thus removed a big source of tension at the conference.

All in all, Yelenevich was rather a risk taker. In Moscow, fighting for the new contract to build Tu-104, he bluffed. During the discussion on the optimal location for the production site of this plane, Yelenevich announced at the board meeting of the Ministry of Aviation Industry that the contract must be given to the Omsk plant. He said the plant could start the assembly of the new aircraft as soon as the next day because preparation for the construction of the new plane was already underway at the plant on its own initiative; even the assembly jigs were already in place, he claimed.

Minister Pyotr Dementyev exploded, "What assembly jigs? What are you telling us here! Nothing of the kind exists! Nobody gave you such orders!"

"I am responsible for my words. If you don't trust me, send a commission, let them check the site," Yelenevich bluffed.

In fact, there were no assembly jigs at the plant. A pile of old jigs and several large test molds for new ones were discarded on the floor by the metal soldering workshop. The next morning the ministry commission would fly to the plant. But the previous night, after Yelenevich's phone call, an emergency shift was announced at the plant. Overnight, the territory of the main assembly workshop was cleared, sills of assembly jigs were brought in and cemented, and some components of assembly jigs were hung. Usually, putting up an assembly jig requires numerous measurements; it takes at least one to two months. This time, a Potemkin village was built in the assembly workshop overnight.

The commission was astonished. The plant got the contract. It then spent about a month dismounting the props and two more months building a proper assembly jig. In the serial design bureau, we received documentation for the systems of the new aircraft, Tu-104. The plant came back to life.

Yelenevich was appointed to be the chairman of the *Sovnarkhoz*.[6] The former chief engineer, Konstantin Golovko, an energetic man, became the plant's director. The plant quickly reached the point of assembling the first copies of the Tu-104, but the plant's airfield was only suitable for aircraft of the smaller Il-28 class. The runway was rather short and old. Chipped cement was patch-coated with asphalt. This was sufficient for an Il-28, but the runway was officially closed to heavier aircraft. Yelenevich took a rather risky step here, too, in nailing down the Tu-104 contract. Despite the ban, he announced that he was going to pay 100,000 rubles to the crew of a Tu-16 (a prototype for Tu-104) to land on our plant's airfield and thereby prove its viability for the larger plane. To appreciate the magnitude of this sum, know that the most luxurious automobile of those days, a ZIM, cost 40,000 rubles at an Omsk car dealership. My monthly salary as a designer was 880 rubles.

Four brave chaps showed up and landed Tu-16 on the plant's airfield. The money for the crew was brought right to the air-stairs. The crew members stuffed it into their pockets, left the plane in the middle of the field without even closing the hatches behind them, and drove away to paint the town red. They returned a couple of days later, completely green. They were still feeling sick when they reached the base of the air-stairs, first lethargically strolling around the aircraft nose and then, one by one, running behind the wheel trolley and bending down to vomit. Then they struggled to climb the ladder into the cockpit, started the engines, and slowly taxied to the runway.

Catastrophes had already happened at this short runway during the period when the plant was producing the Il-28 aircraft. Once, failing to gain the necessary takeoff speed, an Il-28 came down right on the buildings of the plant's village. Now, we would witness the difficulty of a Tu-16 takeoff on an inadequate runway, compounded by the crew's hangovers. As designers who understood the danger and who had seen the crew return in such a drunken state, we held our breath. Could the crew at least see the dashboard? we wondered. Will the pilot blow up the plane too soon, before gaining speed?

After roaring its engines on parking brakes, the plane accelerated quickly: good lift-up. They took off!

After that, this Tu-16 crew, which was in the Omsk region for flight-testing of the onboard radar equipment, was grounded. But it was not possible to disrupt the program of building the new military radars, so this experienced crew got permission to fly again, after strict reprimands. Also, there was a big scandal regarding the expense of 100,000 rubles, but Yelenevich—winner takes all—had quickly hushed that up, through Moscow.

Ultimately, the first jet plane in the world that would offer regular passenger service, Tu-104, would taxi to the runway of the plant's airfield. A lot of people gathered for the event. Before this decisive moment, the crew had been rehearsing the takeoff for some time, rolling the plane up and down the runway.

Acceleration. The plane lifted its nose up. And at the point when powerful gas shafts from the engine pushed against the runway, the asphalt that covered the chipped cement rose up into the air like a black carpet and flew over the aircraft. What would happen to the plane? Asphalt chunks that were scattered around could damage the tail when it came back down. But all went without incident. The numerous spectators were asked to come out and help clear away the asphalt. The plane remained in the air till the runway was free of detritus. After that, the jet landed successfully.

But not everything was successful in the design of the Tu-104. In the aircraft's wing, there was a shaft which turned in order to extend and retract the flaps on the wings. The flaps were key to lift of the wing. The shaft had to rotate properly. It was powered by an electric motor placed in the central part of the wing. The steel shaft was hard to couple during the plane's assembly; experienced assembly experts did it with great effort. The shaft didn't want to bend together with the wing. Deformations were seen clearly on its holding brackets along the wing. Somehow I didn't like it from the very beginning. I thought that, instead of the existing practice of trying to bend the shaft when coupling it, a better idea would be to mount cardan joints, which already existed on the same shaft at places where it entered the wing. The addition of cardan joints would allow the shaft more flexibility.[7]

I went to the head of the serial-production design department, Yuri Allé. He immediately threw water on my idea.

"Don't speak stupidities!" he spouted. "They are not fools sitting at Tupolev's design bureau in Moscow. The plane isn't being built from zero; several hundred Tu-16s have already been produced, and you turn out smarter than everybody? Professor! Go, work, don't stuff your head with nonsense."

We continued to couple the shaft with a tugging effort at the point of assembly. Thus, there was a problem on every completed aircraft, and one day what was due to happen, happened. During a training flight of a Tu-104 near Moscow, this wretched shaft broke when extending the flaps at landing. In this incident, the flap was extended on one wing but not on the second one. The aircraft almost flipped over in the air. The crew quickly spotted the trouble and retracted the flap. The crew was rewarded for being adroit and courageous. But after this, a special committee discovered that the shaft broke because of poor coupling of its components. They checked it all in assembly at the plant in Omsk and discovered the same picture.

The chairman of the Presidium of the Supreme Soviet at that time, Kliment Voroshilov, had flown to Tashkent and back by a Tu-104. He had been offered another plane but refused.

"Does the nation fly by Tu-104?" he had asked.

"It does!"

"Then I will fly too. If you put me in a coffin, you'll be held responsible."

Minister Dementyev was personally standing by the runway at the Vnukovo airport as Voroshilov's plane landed, without a glitch.[8]

A chain of trials was held at the Omsk plant. Qualified assembly experts were accused of low-quality job performance and sacked from the plant. The KGB undertook an investigation. They reached our department.

Allé summoned me, "Here, get acquainted. The comrade from the 'competent authorities' is interested in the reason for the accident. You are a designer; deal with him and explain the matter."

I made several attempts to explain it. Of course, I presented it the same way that I had already tried to present it to my design-bureau boss: the reason is a shortcoming in the design. All the Tu-104 planes were grounded and returned to the plant for a check-up on the shaft coupling. The shaft proved impossible to couple without a bend. Naturally, a serious request was made to Tupolev Design Bureau. A reply followed: the shaft ought to work within the limits of the wing's resiliency. In flight, they insisted, the wing bends upwards, and the shaft's bend should disappear. Possibly this is so in theory.

It was winter, forty degrees below zero Celsius, and a Tu-104 was parked at the open assembly line for checking. At 2:00 a.m., I was called, as a designer.

"Look, designer, the shaft doesn't couple," the workers observed. "Here, you try to couple it; let's see how you manage. . . ."

Lots of other words were said, of an inappropriate kind.

I was wearing an autumn overcoat and light shoes—I simply didn't have any other clothes. Inside, the heat from the airfield heater was like a sauna; assembly workers would wear undershirts. A car drove close with the plant director, Golovko; head of the serial-production design department, Allé; head of the plant technical quality control; and a representative of the military. They had also been called for in the middle of the night. I went outside the hangar, through the hatch. My coat turned to plywood.

"What will you tell us, designer?" Golovko demanded, trying to stand with his back to the wind.

"We have to put in cardan joints, as many as are needed," I insisted.

"Don't speak foolishly, Professor!" Allé exclaimed, pulling his head deeper into his shoulders and pushing his hands down into his pockets. "You already got an answer to this from Moscow."

"Get in!" Golovko directed, diving inside the car. "All seats are taken; Katayev will lie down across our laps. Go!"

We warmed up a little. Golovko turned around and addressed me, "Cardan joints, you say?"

"Yes, cardan joints!"

Allé kicked me with his knee from below and snarled, "You are speaking stupidities again, Professor!"

Golovko paused and asked me, "Well, could you draw these cardan joints for me, the way they should be placed?"

"Of course I could!"

"How much time are you going to need?"

"Two hours."

"It's 2:00 a.m. now. Will you be able to draw them by 7:00 a.m. if we give you a lift to the bureau now?"

"I will."

"Go ahead, draw. For me. A man will come at 7:00 a.m. and pick up the blueprints."

At night, rats ruled the big halls of the design department. They came close, looking at my drawings with interest. I threw anything at them that was at hand, as I toiled through the night. Boris Nepoklonov came at the appointed hour. He had been the head of the group closest to me but had then begun to deal with rocket technology.

"There is something you have to draw and I am to take it to Moscow," he said. "Tell me more."

Already at 2:00 p.m. the next afternoon, Nepoklonov called from Moscow and reported: the blueprints were approved; Andrei Tupolev himself had personally signed them. All previously produced aircraft would have to be upgraded according to these blueprints. This was a victory for me, albeit small.

Apparently, the constructive outcome of the dangerous accident, plus my technical consultations with the KGB representatives, made a good impression somewhere, because the cardan joint affair had an immediate effect.

Allé, my boss in the serial-production design department, summoned me at once. "Seemingly you gave great consultations to KGB," he admitted. "They are now asking to talk to you at the regional department. Go ahead, march there right now; they are waiting; the pass is ordered."

I found the famous, monumental building of the regional department in Omsk and entered the room that was indicated on my pass. Three officers sat at a table.

"Hello. My name is Katayev. Came by invitation," I stated.

The officer at the desk by the window raised his head and inquired, "Are you to see me? Good day. What's that on your eyes?"

"Why are you interested? Eyeglasses. Shortsighted."

"Well, it's not so bad."

"Yes, indeed, I've worn glasses for a long time, got used to it."

"They are so big and pretty."

"Just that I failed to buy an appropriate frame, so I made a frame from acrylic plastic to my taste."

"How very interesting! We would like to know you better."

My biography took thirty seconds. Most likely, they had read it more than once at the plant's human resources department.

"How are your relations with comrades at work?" the officer asked.

I replied that I had had no conflicts with anybody so far.

"We want to propose that you change jobs and work at the authorities of state security. What would you say?"

"My view is sharply negative! I am not going to!"

"Why so sharp and hasty? Think it over, consider all pros and cons."

"I am not even going to think about it. My goal is to be a designer. I understand something about it and can do some things. I have been aiming at this all my conscious life. I don't need another job. Thanks for your confidence. I am not going!"

"Wow! You are a stubborn comrade."

"True, especially when I feel that I'm right."

"Shame, shame. Do you live in the group residence?"

"Yes, I am a bachelor."

"Who are your roommates?"

"There have been many, but lately just two of us. The other's a school classmate."

"What kind of person is your classmate? Can you describe him?"

"Of course I can—he is my friend. He is a solid man, amiable. He employs workers who are kicked out from other workshops. And they do a triple load of work for him. They invite him to their weddings. He has a *bayan,* and I have an accordion—we are popular.[9] The head of the workshop treats him like his son. And I wouldn't be friends with him if he were a lousy man."

"So you give him a top grade. And what do you think: Would he agree to come work for us?"

"Well, you would have to offer it to him yourself. I don't know."

"Can you pass on my offer to him to come by for a talk?"

"I will. When should he come?"

"Same time tomorrow."

"I'll tell him."

"Success to you in the field of design. Good luck!"

In the evening, I passed on the offer to my friend. He didn't have to think even for a minute.

"I'm going to go," my roommate asserted. "They have an interesting job there. They need aviation specialists, too. I will. Tomorrow I'll say yes."

My friend graduated from the KGB school, worked in Omsk and Moscow, dealt with plane hijacking, became head of the Ryazan KGB department, then major-general. Now he's retired. Our families became friends for life.

By that time, the Omsk Civil Aviation Plant had begun serial production of the R-12 rocket from the Dnepropetrovsk design bureau. Some of the designers were moved to this terribly secret job. Work on the Tu-104 was in decline. I started to teach aviation subjects at the city technical college for aviation, graduated some students, and kept pulling the yoke for the Council of Young Specialists.

The college gave me students to train at the plant. I had to think up ways to keep them busy for a month. I decided to use their help to make a superglider, a water vessel with a pulsating jet engine. I had accumulated experience with this from my own school days. We connected two parallel 5-meter-long hollow skis to underwater wings. The fuel tank block and the engine were behind the pilot's seat. We successfully tested the vessel in the plant's fountain, but without starting the jet engine. Later, I calculated that the drag of the permanently pulsating engine could outweigh the glider together with the pilot, in which case I would have blown up in it! The boys from DOSAAF begged me to give the superglider to them and simply mounted an ordinary outboard boat motor on it.[10]

Eventually, the time came to have a family. I saw my wife-to-be for the first time at the Omsk factory. She worked as a technologist in the rubber containers workshop. I thought she looked like a TV actress of that time. She was bouncy and pretty. There she strolls, in my mind's eye, waving her schoolbag, paying no attention to her destiny standing by the side of the road, watching her.

"Aha," I said to myself, "one interesting girl!"

Later, I ran into her many times at parties at the club of the Baranov Aviation Engines Plant in Omsk. My pal Yuri and I would stand by a column in the club watching dancing pairs and appraising the girls: that one seems ok but a little fat. This one's legs are crooked; that one's teeth . . . and so on. Sometimes, we arranged special meetings. We would invite a girl of our taste for detailed inspection, and we wouldn't let on which one of us had initiated the encounter. We treated these girls strictly as gentlemen would; nothing improper was permitted.

Yuri finished the KGB school and ended his bachelor life. He found his future wife in Sverdlovsk, whence she had escaped pesky admirers from the town of Rustavi, Georgian Socialist Republic. Of course, I went to his wedding, and later he came to mine with his young wife. I married Galina—that girl I used to see in the street—in 1958. Around this time, the Omsk Civil Aviation Plant was getting more and more involved in the rocket business. And at the same time, conversations began to circulate about the production of a second missile, the R-14, in Dnepropetrovsk. My inner voice began to bug me again: Dnepropetrovsk started to look like a good possibility. Then, as it happened, when visiting my parents in Perm during summer vacation in 1958, I accidentally ran into my boyhood classmate Vadim Varyvdin at the railway station.

"Oooh! We managed to meet after all this time!" Vadim exclaimed. "Eight years! Where are you working now?"

"I'm at an aircraft factory in Omsk, doing aviation design."

"And I'm in Dnepropetrovsk, I work with antennae. Come and visit sometime. Your Omsk guys come to us."

"What's the city like?"

"Miraculous. Green. The Dnieper is a marvel. Beaches. A southern city!"[11]

"And the plant?"

"The plant is enormous, but I am at the design bureau. The job is very interesting."

"Maybe I'll come down."

"Do come, Nina and I will be glad to see you. She's known you for a long time, remembers you from school parties. Here's my address. Bye!"

"Bye!"

And so, together with my wife, we decided to roll a test ball into my dream city. We wrote to Mikhail Yangel, the chief designer, that we were two engineers who would like to work at the design bureau. The letter reached the addressee. I later saw his signed note on this letter: "I agree to take both of them." They sent us questionnaires to fill in, but we would not leave Omsk for another two years or so.

In 1960, our daughter was born. On the day, I made a phone call to the maternity ward from the office of my boss, Allé. He had people there. Everybody was waiting, interested in what the outcome would be. The answer came. Allé was the first to comment.

"Judging by your unhappy expression, I conclude that it's a girl!" he said. "Did I guess right?"

"Yes, . . ." I forced out. A transition to a new station in life: I was a husband. Now I was also a father, the father of little Marina.

I didn't tell them that we hadn't even thought of a boy's name: we had had a firm plan for a girl. My wife, Galina, and I were very careful and systematic in this process, and all exterior parameters were realized exactly as planned. I couldn't have even supposed that it would be possible to be so exact in programming human looks.

I was very lucky with my mother-in-law and Galina's stepfather. I still retain good memories of them. Her stepfather came from the start into a family with three little girls; he replaced their dad, who had perished in the war, and another child, a half brother, was born. They also reared a nephew and helped relatives in the village. It was a hardworking family of friends.

All my classmates in school got married around this time, too. We managed to turn a group residence into a new families' residence. Every month a new little tenant appeared. If one month was sterile, then the next month twins would be born. Baby diapers hung everywhere. Fueled by a desire to give some extra warmth to babies in a frosty Siberian winter, minifires and floods broke out in the residence now and again from home engineering efforts. Once, the corridor's ceiling crashed down, heavy with the moisture of endless diapers. The issue of repairs to the whole residence of young families arose. Relocation might have been the answer—but where? The plant's housing program was too tight.

At that time, the plant started so-called "wages adjustment." My salary had been raised twice since 1956, and by then I was making one thousand rubles a month.[12] I worked without any spare time and grabbed every job I could.

Once, Allé directed, "You like everything new, go make a flight container to transfer the stage props of the Omsk Choir. They are planning to go abroad, so the container must satisfy international standards. They need it in one week."

The Omsk Choir stage-props manager came to me at the main room of the design bureau and demonstratively fell on his knees in front of me. All my colleagues' jaws dropped. Young ladies used to cry here to push for a flat; young men cursed everybody in the world, also because of the housing question. But nothing of this kind had happened until now.

"Young man!" he pleaded. "Your boss said that you alone can do it. I beg you by Christ and our Lord: we're on fire, they will cancel our trip! First trip abroad! If you don't build it, they will kick me out! Save me!"

Another time I had to connect the switch of a new washing machine that the plant started producing on the basis of the British Hoovermatic, with the Omsk city emblem on it. I also worked on designing light aluminum furniture, and table-sized gift models of Tu-104, and cast-iron railings, and lots of other things. I worked without saying no. Apparently, for this reason, the notification of "wages adjustment" read that my salary would be 1,300 rubles. I signed the agreement. The money was less important than moving forward. But when payday came, it turned out that my salary was set at 1,100 rubles. What was the matter? I went to Allé. He took a long time to breathe noisily through his nose and stare out the window.

"You know," he said finally. "It's kind of awkward: to pay the same salary to old men who went to the front and came back as is paid to you, a young man. For you, everything is still ahead."

"If it were so from the beginning, there would be no question," I retorted. "I would've understood. But you did it secretly!"

In the evening, I went for an appointment with the new plant director, Yakov Kolupayev. Unlike his predecessor, loud-voiced Golovko, this guy had the looks of an opera tenor and spoke in a thin voice. His appearance completely clashed with the obscene talk that was in use at the plant. I wrote my name down in the appointments book with the director's secretary. I entered last and sat at the table in front of the director.

"Why do you sit here? Sit where you usually sit," he insisted. "This is the place for people who come by appointment."

"I came by appointment."

"Stop playing with my mind, you could have come anytime you needed. Next one!"

"I am the next one. There's nobody else; I am last."

"Such timing!"

"I have an official appointment. I wrote it down in the book."

The head of the party organization of the plant, the head of the trade union, the deputy director for personnel, and the head of the labor and wages department all looked on with interest, waiting to see what would happen next.

"And what do you want?" the director demanded.

"This is my statement," I replied. "I am asking for a flat, this time for myself. My family has grown larger. And I am not pleased that the salary was not handled very decently."

"Here sits the head of labor and wages. I am passing the instruction on to him. Consider the problem fixed. Done!"

"No, not done. The main question: housing."

"How many flats have you distributed to young specialists?"

"Eighty-six flats in three years."

"What a fool! You should have distributed one to yourself first. And now there isn't any housing. I cannot promise. I won't lie to you."

"What are you teaching me, to grab things for myself? Families needed flats, and I was single. Now I also have a family."

"Rent a place in a private sector, live there now, and then we'll see."

"I rented a place in a private sector once. My wife is still sick from it."

"Choose another one."

"May I say a word?" the deputy director for personnel interjected. "Do you trust me?"

"So far I have no reason not to," I responded.

"This time I won't fail you either. You will have a flat in May!"

"Then you sort it out yourself!" rejoined Kolupayev, passing my case to the deputy director for personnel. "You promise too much!"

"Very good. Thank you!" I said, quickly making for the exit before they changed their minds.

We had a small celebration at home to mark this successful talk. We began to make plans. A flat! Our own! Only someone who has waited for one for a long time can appreciate what this means. On the other hand, Dnepropetrovsk still lay at the backs of our minds. Galina was already infected with my dream, too. We decided: let's wait and see.

Construction on the new housing in Omsk went on all year round. Despite special additives, the cement solution still froze during the winter. To prevent the solution from melting in the spring under strong sun, a winter-built building was usually painted white. We went to look at it: the house was already completed during the winter. Here it was—our home! It was red brick, painted with some white patches. This was a bad whitening job! The April sun warmed the solution, it melted, and the five-story brick building slid in different directions and ultimately collapsed. Only side walls up to the second floor remained standing. The building's guard was lucky: he had gone to buy bread shortly before the catastrophe and so wasn't buried under debris.

As for us? How should we evaluate this crashing of hopes? Was it an ending or a new beginning?

I went to the plant's deputy director for personnel. He spread his hands.

"Force majeure! The housing picture is totally unclear now," he conceded.

"Then it looks like we will have to resign and leave," I announced.

"What? You have such a firm standing here. Where will you go? Everybody knows you here, and you will have to start everything anew elsewhere. Besides, housing is in shortage everywhere!"

A letter from Dnepropetrovsk came. Human resources informed us that I would be given a job, but there was no word about my wife. At a family meeting, we decided: I would go to Dnepropetrovsk;

Galina, with the child, would go to Perm to stay with my parents and would come to Dnepropetrovsk at my call.

I went to Kolupayev with a resignation statement and bumped into him on the stairs; he was catching a business flight. The deputy director for personnel walked with him and blocked my way.

"Here you are," the deputy director for personnel exclaimed with surprise when he saw me. "Yakov Vasilyevich," he then announced to Kolupayev, "Katayev is going to quit!"

Kolupayev turned to me without stopping.

"Forget it!" he bellowed at me. "And you," he commanded the deputy director for personnel, "Don't sign his resignation!"

The chief engineer remained behind to act as director. I went to him at 10:00 p.m. with a resignation statement, quitting on my own.

"What are you thinking?" the chief engineer demanded. "Go, good-bye! I won't sign anything!"

"Then, according to a new legislation it is my right not to show up at work two weeks from now. I registered my statement in the book as of today."

"And then what?"

"Then I don't work, and I am paid my salary at the expense of the person guilty of not signing my resignation."

"No kidding! Listen," he asked the head of the labor and wages department, who looked inside, "Is it true this law exists?"

"Yes, it's a recent law," his colleague confirmed.

"All right, you will probably return to us. After some suffering, you'll come back," the chief engineer predicted. "Here, I am signing it! Bye!"

CHAPTER 2

Yuzhnoye Design Bureau

On June 1, 1960, two weeks after my resignation from the Omsk Civil Aviation Plant, I arrived at Dnepropetrovsk. I found the house of Vadim Varyvdin near the train station. Picture it: the door of apartment number 24 is open. A young barefoot woman is washing the floor. She looks up at me and recognizes me at once.

"Good morning!" she sings out. "By what winds do you come here?"

"Well, . . . I think by good ones. My wife and I have decided to move here."

"Perfect! Our Perm cohort has an opening! Let's call Vadim at work now. He'll be so happy! Come in, make yourself at home!"

From that day on, the Varyvdins would be our closest and truest friends.

When he arrived back home, Vadim wrapped me in his embrace and immediately outlined the situation at the design bureau.

"The design department is an elite one at the bureau. Ask for a job there. Let me get you a meeting with one of their designers. Erik Kashanov is a good fellow. He'll tell you everything. Wait for a phone call. Until you find a flat, live with us."

"Stay as long as you need," Nina concurred. "The couch is yours. And today we have an excuse to celebrate—your arrival!"

Nina was working at a school teaching English and German at the time, but she was also an expert on tasty snacks and dishes.

Certainly, Vadim and I remembered our school days. Perm school number 9, for boys, was not only famous for having the strongest volleyball team, which our classmates joined, but also for having its own jazz band. Imagine a jazz band in a Soviet school of the 1940s, when puritanism meant not only separate education but was even taken to the point of measuring the width of pant legs! Together with Vadim, I had played accordion in this band. We had even been assigned a duet. We remembered how the band chaps dragged me and my accordion to all the schools for girls, where we gave real concerts. Garik Renae shone at playing the piano. His performance of Liszt's Hungarian Rhapsody was perfect. At audience request, Garik was able to perform a headache on a piano, or a sick stomach, or extreme surprise. Girls at parties were frozen-hypnotized by Boris Litvinenko singing "Just Say I Love Her" while looking at his beloved sitting in the front row.[1] Female soloists in the band were chosen not for their voices but for their legs. The key number (and this at school!) was the guys' stylized dance to the band's music and sung operetta strophes from Paul Abraham's *Ball at the Savoy* (1932):

> He who's cruelly in love must know the law of the Orient—
> We must jealously protect our wives.
> Let her not spend time with anybody:
> A wife's place is at her husband's harem.

Vadim and I reminisced about our classmates till midnight, and, in the morning, we went to plant number 586 together.[2] The reception at the personnel department was warm.

"You've arrived? Very good," the personnel representative said. "Get a residence certificate and come over to us. How does one get a residence certificate, you may ask? Finding housing is your problem. We don't have housing, and you are not a young specialist any longer. Search."

I searched for a long time. Nobody wanted to take a family with a child as tenants. Surprisingly, I got help thanks to my good relations with ordinary landing-gear workers from the workshop in Omsk.

"Are you on a business trip, too?" they asked when they ran into me at the plant checkpoint.

"Well, I came for good. Can't find a flat. They don't take a family with a child."

"We'll fix this for you! We stay near here, at a grandfather's place. We'll pour alcohol into him till he agrees."

Indeed, my kind worker friends plied the grandfather with alcohol all day and eventually got his consent. We would become good friends with Timofei Nikiforovich—granddad Timofei—and his wife, grandma Pasha, and would remain on good terms for many years.

Finally, with all kinds of procedures taken care of, I walked through my secret dream checkpoint, past young soldiers, and onto the territory of plant number 586. I liked everything there right away. It was a garden of a plant, with people dressed in casual, warm-weather clothes and workshops much bigger than we had had in Omsk.

Vladimir Kovtunenko welcomed me to my new job in the design department (at that time he was just the head of this design department, not an academician yet). I liked him at once.

"A new guy? Hello!" he greeted me, stretching out his hand, which was a bit deformed by a war injury. "A graduate of what institute?"

"I am not a young specialist anymore."

"But not from Dnepropetrovsk State University?"

"No. From Kazan Aviation Institute. And why are you so much against the university?"

"Because the university prepares specialists with narrow training, but the Kazan institute, for example, gives a broad training to specialists; that's why they are so valuable. You say you dealt with hydraulics in Omsk? Then go start working on pneumatic hydro systems of engine systems in Kukushkin's sector."

Very young guys were working in that sector. They understood something about rockets; they had been well oriented. A rocket for me was an entirely new topic. At first, I had to learn the blueprints and scrape tracing paper, as I had done in Omsk. Later, the job got more interesting, but clarity with regard to many details did not come until much later.

In the early 1960s, an ambitious race started between the Soviet Union and the United States: Who would be the first to land on the moon? Just as the first manned space flight on the R-7 rocket had been, the moon program was allocated to Sergei Korolyov's Test and Design Bureau No. 1. The booster and the whole moon space system was to be built anew. This project was given a code name, N-1.

The moon-landing program became financially unbearable for the Soviet economy, and an intensive search for ways to reduce expenses began. The initial data that had been put into the draft project envisaged the building of a transportation system to take the recoverable spacecraft to the moon's orbit and a lunar landing module of seventy tons. This weight was deemed acceptable for the lander, which was dealt with at Vladimir Barmin's design bureau.

Accepting this weight might have saved the program a little money, but for some reason, then-available information about the American works was not taken into account; their weight of a lunar spaceship was approximately half that accepted by the Soviet program. Perhaps the most important issue not addressed: the reasons why our aircraft, rocket, and satellite takeoff payload ratios were twice as big as the foreign ones. His Majesty the Working Class has always put its imprint on the most brilliant scientific and engineering solutions in the Soviet Union, starting from ore mining. For this reason, we mostly achieved the necessary consumer quality of Soviet equipment through quantity and often, as in the case of the lander, this resulted in added weight.

Already in Omsk I was trying to understand: Why did the first passenger jet plane in the world, Tu-104, have a maximal payload of only 7 percent of its flight weight while the French Caravelle, for which serial production began at the same time, in 1958, had a 15 percent maximal payload? I privately concluded that the reason was that the existing design solutions from the Tu-16 bomber had been used for the civilian aircraft. But this was not so. The limitation was the result of the low quality of our technologies and materials. Even by this most primitive comparative analysis of all flying aircraft—Soviet and foreign—our piloted lunar craft was to have a weight at least twice that of the American one.

Ignoring our low level of technological potential was the fatal error that from the very beginning put a cross on the whole Soviet lunar program. Frankly, it could not be realized. Still, some measures were taken. The very first calculations showed that a spaceship with a weight of seventy tons would not ensure a landing of two cosmonauts on the moon. The head of the division at the Rocket Armaments Main Department, Aleksei Kalashnikov, a military man, went to see Korolyov and showed him materials obtained from a number of research institutes. Calculations showed that the lunar spaceship would weigh no less than 150 to 170 tons. Thus, the capacity of the rocket booster had to be increased. This was a serious obstacle. There would not be enough weight even for one cosmonaut's landing on the moon's surface.

Korolyov got anxious and summoned a meeting. The name of academician Mstislav Keldysh, for some reason, was voiced as the main argument at the meeting. "Keldysh said that the accepted weight will be sufficient" became a mantra. Keldysh's authority as "space industry theoretician" turns out to be higher than engineers' calculations, apparently. However, disagreements between Korolyov and the military were not closed at this. Pushy Kalashnikov brought his doubts to the head of the Rocket Armaments Main Department, Anatoly Semyonov.

"Indeed, the matter is too serious," Semyonov quavered. "To start with, let us receive and compare the exact parameters of our rocket and the American moon program's rocket, Saturn V, and then calculate it one more time. The project is too far along. We need to know everything for sure . . . and fast."

They instantly wrote down the request, and it was signed by the head of the Soviet General Staff of the Armed Forces headquarters. To speed up the reply, the ciphered cable was sent straight to the Soviet ambassador in Washington, Anatoly Dobrynin, bypassing subordinates. The ambassador gave a quick answer: the Americans are making a lunar spacecraft of 150 to 170 tons.

Kalashnikov took Dobrynin's reply to Korolyov again. He read the ciphered note and sat for a long time, holding his head.

"Keldysh has let me down! But whatever, let's do the job!"

Thereafter, Korolyov managed to slightly raise the load capacity of the N-1 rocket to lift a lunar craft of 120 tons. Although our spaceship had no specific shape yet, it was still obvious that this weight was catastrophically insufficient for landing a man on the moon.

It is possible that the virus of doubting the N-1 capabilities did not infect the military alone. Either by command or out of initiative—I had no way of knowing which at that time—Mikhail Yangel's design bureau in Dnepropetrovsk got busy, too. The Yangel-Glushko clan decided to challenge the Korolyov-Kuznetsov clan. In 1960, the design bureau in Dnepropetrovsk started an analytical study of their safety-net variant of a big booster with 100 tons of payload. The rocket was called the RK-100. The idea was to eventually increase its payload up to 150 tons and more. Valentin Glushko offered his large engines for this rocket.

But what should be done with the N-1 rocket? Design bureaus and plants with thousands of employees had been spun up. And the parameters for the rocket had an error! Who would stand responsible? Keldysh? Korolyov? But they were beyond responsibility. The minister? But he had been let down by technicians. And who had let the technicians down? The equipment. Let's blame everything on it.

A campaign to discredit the N-1 began. The rocket used liquid-propellant engines from Nikolai Kuznetsov, whose design bureau had extensive experience with building jet engines for military and civilian aircraft. At that time, these engines were installed on the strategic bomber Tu-95, its passenger modification, Tu-114, and many other aircraft. Kuznetsov's engines were always outstanding for their degree of reliability, exactly what was required for a piloted space flight. Even now, forty years on, it can be seen that the choice of that design bureau was fully justified, despite its limited experience in liquid-propellant rocket engines at that time. But the patriarch of liquid-propellant engines, Glushko, interpreted the choice of Kuznetsov's engines as a sign of mistrust and a personal insult. There were thirty-six engines on the N-1 rocket altogether. This very fact was used by Glushko, Barmin, and the designer of instrumentation for the control system, Kuznetsov. They signed a letter to the Central Committee in which they cast in doubt all the work on the N-1, saying that "it's not a rocket but a warehouse of engines."

The N-1 rocket had accidents in the first three launches. This was bound to happen in the space-race climate of that time. It was necessary to rush to the testing range and make a report to superiors, at the expense of lab and bench tests. Superiors in Moscow could not grasp why bench tests take so long. "When are you bringing the machine to the launchpad? Why the delay? Whose fault is it? You take too long. Hurry up! We are behind the Americans! You don't get the political importance of this task": such hectoring accompanied almost all the work. Naturally, this didn't contribute to its quality.

But the main issue was that we were hopelessly stuck. Thundering resolutions of the Politburo, issued just a week before the Americans flew to the moon, to carry out the N-1 development at takeover speed, could not substitute for the powerful technical potential which the Soviet Union lacked and which the United States possessed. But nobody dared admit this. That's why everybody was just waiting for a convenient chance. The chance presented itself. The complex N-1 rocket, hammered together against the background noise of demands from above, failed to fly. After the first three failed launches, the accidents were blamed on Kuznetsov's engines, and the N-1 project was closed down. But it was not the engines' fault: in the rivalry between the two military-economic systems, the might of one of the powers was greater than that of the other.

Gradually, work on the alternative rocket, RK-100, at Dnepropetrovsk burnt out. While involved in it, I got some experience as a designer of a system and made friends with people involved in all the services of the design bureau. Noticing my special interest in design, the head of my group, Valentin Kovalchuk, once said, "Why don't you take up an interesting problem: valves for fuel tanks. Rockets are getting bigger, and tanks are now big, too. They require safety valves with a gas flow rate of approximately one kilogram per second. Our valve department makes valves the size of a bucket. A rocket valve must not be bigger than a one- or two-liter glass jar."

After this, I had a long discussion with him about the design of a double-action valve. I drafted it all and made calculations. I submitted my drafts to the factory. Then, for the first time, I ran into the peculiar Ukrainian job culture. My good friends, the workers from Omsk who had come here on a business trip, tried to explain it to me. It took them four hours to do a job that took the workers here in Dnepropetrovsk a week to accomplish. The locals threatened to pull the Omsk guys limb from limb and forced them to leave, but they were not in a hurry to work here anyway. Compared to the Siberian tempo of work, the Ukrainians were about ten times slower. At every stage of manufacture in the Dnepropetrovsk factory, they explained to me at length how the valve would be made in three months, or six months, or perhaps in a year's time.

"And what do you want?" they demanded, "that we should drop everything and get busy with your valves? We'll make it when its turn comes. Call on us in a month, ask how it's going. . . ."

I found blueprints at the valve workshop and asked the technologist to give them to a lathe operator. I met the lathesmith and explained to him what this gizmo was—a double-action valve—how it works, where it goes, and why it should be made ASAP. I came over to the workshop to chat with this young guy twice more. A week later the valve was ready.

After this, we found a large tank in the workshop and decided to test the valve there, as envisaged by blueprints. But with the emission of a kilo of air per second, the tank and valve would be like a bomb—a bomb inside the workshop. We started testing. With the first emissions from the valve at the frequency of two to three seconds, the walls of the workshop and windows with glass immediately caught resonance and began to oscillate. The plant's bosses came running and found who was guilty—it was me. But the job was done. All the rockets built by the design bureau began to use this valve, and it later became the subject of the thesis of one of the designers from the valve department.

At the same period of time, work on building an orbital combat rocket started. First, a nuclear warhead would be taken into orbit, and then, at the needed moment, a signal would crash it down upon the enemy's head. A request was made to test the start of the engine of the rocket's orbiting reentry vehicle in conditions of an

orbit flight—in zero gravity. My experience of working at Omsk Civil
Aviation Plant came in handy here.

I proposed using my homeland passenger aircraft Tu-104 to create a zero gravity regime during its flight along a specially chosen
trajectory. I went to the Flight Research Institute in Zhukovsky.[3] An
aircraft-maker myself, I canvassed aircraft-makers on their understanding of all technical issues. We determined the general scheme
of operations for this test and how to accomplish it despite the dangers. Sometimes engines blew up when tested on a rig. We found a
method of preventing a possible explosion of the engine. All experiments ran successfully. A number of quick-thinking chaps, as well
as my boss in the design department, received invention patents
for these tests.

During the year of work in the Yuzhnoye Design Bureau, I suc-
ceeded in pushing forward two projects that in essence were not
related to my designer's job: sending technologists from the plant
in Dnepropetrovsk to Omsk to master the pattern method of tailor-
ing large-plate rocket parts, as well as organizing an operation and
maintenance service for rockets modeled on a similar service at the
Omsk Civil Aviation Plant. Thus, I was constantly sticking my nose
into other people's business. But the results were visible, most certainly to me, and this brought about not only satisfaction but also
new contacts with people and friendly informal relations.

CHAPTER 3

The Nedelin Disaster

Another important event of 1960 would end some lives and change many others, including my own. Missile accidents are not rare, but I would like to tell the story of this most horrible accident in the history of missile technology as it was told to me by colleagues at that time.

It was October 24, 1960, and the desert sun at the Baikonur test range, in present-day Kazakhstan, was still in full heat. The asphalt and concrete were hot. Of course, it's not the middle of a desert summer, when a thermometer a meter away from cement shows eighty degrees Celsius, but it was still hot. At launching pad No. 42, a peculiar picture could be seen even from the gate: against the grey and yellow pastel colors of the landscape, a slim, white obelisk soared above everything, pointing up into a pure blue cold sky. This was the R-16 missile on a launchpad on a little hill.

A stumpy Kazakh—a soldier at the checkpoint—censoriously inspected a slip of paper with a stamp—the pass into the test range. All the employees of the checkpoint services at the test range were Kazakhs. Unlike good-humored and compliant Russians, the Kazakhs served at all control points like robots; it was impossible to convince them that you had forgotten to bring the pass and would definitely show it tomorrow. If you have a pass—then go in, walk or drive. If not—then the way is closed. Launchpad passes were issued only according to a restricted list, which was typed up and signed by the local military command on a single sheet of paper. This list was then constantly amended with handwritten scribbles, on both sides.

To a casual observer, it would be impossible to understand why this slim white obelisk so powerfully lured people. They tried to get to it by hook or by crook. Probably people were first of all enticed by a desire to be at least some part of a sacred rite for this white deity that forced them to travel thousands of kilometers away from home into a desert, that deprived them of months of time they could spend being with their relatives or just thinking about something other than the unpredictable behavior of this capricious, almost live creature that robbed young men of the best years of their own lives.

The white obelisk was a dangerous creature indeed. It would be filled with 130 tons of fuel, almost to the top: this fuel would inflame violently, almost explode, with a beastly roar and groan. This hellish invention of chemists, made out of almost innocent products used for fertilization, would then be ready, with an all-deafening roar, to carry this white obelisk higher and higher till it disappeared, melted away in front of the eyes of all the slaves and patricians clustered around this latter-day arena—the sand dunes around the launchpad.

The sound of a reserve diesel generator was hammering at the launch platform, and the sweetened smoke of diesel oil occasionally reached the launchpad. This sound was dominant for the time being. Other sounds sank into the immense vastness of the desert: there were too few items around to reflect sound.

Test operators ran up to the fuel-filled missile now and again. For their convenience, an old cabin on wheels was placed near the launch platform. This cabin had promptly come to be known as a "bank-bus." There were railings behind the cabin and an eight-meter shaft further behind—underneath was a concrete-paved area and the entrance to rooms located under the launcher. The bank-bus was usually pulled away before the launch.

The R-16 missile that was standing at the launchpad was one of the first heavy strategic missiles. It presented its makers with lots of unexpected surprises, particularly in electrical circuitry.

On this day, the missile was almost launched. The "membranes' rupture" button was pressed. On this command, pyrocharges broke through very thick membranes separating engines from tanks. Then the "launch" button was pressed, but the missile refused to fly. Its electronic brains had failed to understand something. What exactly? It was necessary to find out. That's why a pile of electric-circuit diagrams were brought into the bank-bus. Lots of people crowded inside; it got hot even though all the windows in front of the desk in the bank-bus were taken out.

In the shade of the missile, on a chair between the missile and bank-bus, sat the commander-in-chief of the Strategic Rocket Forces, Deputy Minister of Defense Marshal Mitrofan Nedelin, as he attentively listened to the arguments and shouting between designers. The bosses in Moscow demanded daily personal reports from the commander-in-chief of the Strategic Rocket Forces on the progress of testing the new strategic missile that was capable of lifting the most powerful hydrogen bomb. A missile with this charge was a major trump card in a big international political game to determine who had a thicker strategic club.

The marshal was not amused. Boris Stroganov, representative of the party's Central Committee and head of the subdivision of rocket and missile technology, called Moscow after a failed launch and spoke to Konstantin Rudnev, the chairman of the State Committee of the Council of Ministers for Defense Technology, saying that the missile standing at the launcher now, in his opinion, must not be launched at all; the fuel must be drained and all the defects manifested at the launch must be sorted out in detail. The marshal wanted to sort out personally whether this was the case indeed. I can imagine Nedelin thinking to himself, "Has the Central Committee started undermining me?"

There must be no mistakes with this missile. A successful launch is such a plus to a rocket-supervising marshal. It would be as if he lifted the darned thing into the sky with his own hands. What if the launch goes haywire? Then he would have to hunch down on a carpet in Moscow, both at Minister Rudnev's office and at the

Central Committee. And I'm sure the marshal felt that they would never understand up there how complex a launch is.

Lots of academicians arrived to watch the launch, including Aleksandr Ishlinsky and Boris Petrov.

"Is this a circus or what?" the marshal might have wondered to himself. "And this 'central commitnik' Stroganov, who noses around everywhere, muttering, 'too many defects. . . .' Yet if I listen to him they are going to say, 'The marshal was sheepish, he was bridle-reined by a Central Committee bureaucrat. Didn't take steps to accelerate. . . .' And the academicians, what are they here for? The main people now are these shaggy guys in the bank-bus. I wonder what these guys understand in this drawing like a plate of spaghetti? They are all like teenagers, and such a complicated thing was trusted to them. Must I track those worn-out blueprints with my own finger?"

It was hard to make any sense of the noise coming from inside the bank-bus. However, demands to launch the missile could be understood from sporadic outcries.

The launch ramp, which was on a steep hillock of the launching pad, was well ventilated. The skeleton structure of the launching table allowed a breeze to sweep around. Marshal Nedelin took off his dress cap and began to help the breeze dry his slightly wet underarms with light waves of his hand. The clerk's chair he was sitting in was slightly creaking in unison with the movement of the marshal's cap.

Taking advantage of the pause, generals from launching pad No. 1 approached the marshal with paperwork, together with the head of the test range, Konstantin Gerchik. The test range was getting ready to launch cosmonaut No. 2 from the second launching pad; their lives were going along as usual. And here was the marshal, right here, close by. Why not make use of this opportunity to resolve some administrative problems of the test range with the marshal? Lev Grishin, deputy chairman of the State Committee of the Council of Ministers for Defense Technology, was helping the military brass from the space launching pad, mostly by echoing them.

For some reason, it was suitable to do all this in the shade of a filled-up missile that was carrying electrical current in the process of testing, with torn membranes and rocket engines already filled with volatile fuel.

The marshal reluctantly took the papers one by one, looked through them, holding them on his knee. But mostly he strained his ears to hear the noise and shouts from the bank-bus. The main question for him was being decided there now: to launch or not to launch a missile.

Some distance from the launch platform, outside its perimeter, a little trench had been dug out as a lookout for VIPs. The top of the trench had been covered with a concrete slab. Nedelin had personally gone to inspect the structure and hadn't liked it.

"What did you put the slab there for?" he had demanded. "To smash us down with in case of an accident? Remove the slab!"

The slab had been hastily removed.

This day's VIPs—academicians—somehow seemed out of place at the launchpad. They concluded everything was progressing toward a launch and decided to look at the place where they were going to observe it. Nedelin asked Boris Stroganov to look after the academicians. Stroganov hesitated.

"I'd like to see the outcome of the check-ups," he protested.

Ishlinsky reacted right away.

"Good, you are now our manager," he said. "We cannot go to the observation lookout without you. And you want to stay behind. That's not the way! Do come with us."

Stroganov agreed to go, grudgingly.

At the launchpad, test operators from Dnepropetrovsk, together with designers of the control system of the missile from Test and Design Bureau 692 at Kharkov, were still trying to catch yet another error in the documents. Shrewd and obstinate in his job, Vladimir Sergeyev, deputy chief designer of the Kharkov design bureau, raced a whole crowd of designers to the launchpad. In the course of examination, everything narrowed down to some bugs in the electric-circuit blueprints.

Passions inside the bank-bus were heating up. Gas masks, a compulsory accessory of each specialist present at the launchpad, were thrown into a corner, tangled underfoot, or pushed under the table.

The blueprint was viciously slammed into its place. Someone would point a finger at the drawing, demanding to "switch it on"; that finger would be intercepted in the air by a dissenter. Voices began to turn husky from all the shouting. The breeze was creasing the yellow-orange blueprint of the electric circuits, worn out with all this finger poking.

From the hillock, the marshal had a comfortable view. Yangel calmly strolled nearby, occasionally gesticulating: he was trying to persuade Aleksandr Mrykin, head of the Main Directorate for Missile Weapons, of something. Yangel had celebrated his forty-ninth birthday two days previously. Naturally, all the toasts and well-wishing had mostly dealt with his creation, the R-16 missile standing at the launchpad now.

The work at the side of the missile continued apace. Kostya Luarsabov, slightly shy of the marshal sitting on a chair next to him, was fussing near the launching table. As the engine expert, he was concerned with checking and rechecking, again and again, to make sure that the pipes of the launch device were properly connected to the missile. Local military handymen had been able to put together pipes of different threading and diameter, as they had done before.

Luarsabov saw a gust of wind sweep the dust around the missile and bend the brim of Yangel's straw hat up. The hat jumped and rolled along the concrete road. Yangel turned around and trotted after it.

At that moment, there was a rumble at the top of the missile.

Luarsabov sensed this rumble, familiar from rig testing, under his skin: the engine of the fueled missile had started—up there, at the second stage. His legs automatically sprang away from the launch table. Bending down, he dived out of a rapidly falling rust-brown cloud, as drops of acid from the upper tank of disintegrating missile slapped his bald spot.

Dozens of tons of fuel and oxidizer merged within seconds into a joint explosion, making two clouds—one went up in a fiery mushroom, while the second one, curling around under its rim, swirled on the ground away from the missile.

Luarsabov ran. He knew: the right way to run from a lethal cloud is into the wind. But his head was not controlling his actions; his legs simply carried him towards the exit from the launchpad. The cloud was chasing him. His torso and head went in front; his legs ran behind, barely catching up. As Luarsabov ran, he groaned with despair. In seconds, the cloud of smoke and fire hid both the marshal and the bank-bus crowded with designers and test operators. Soldiers fell from the top of the cloud or jumped down onto the concrete of the pre-table area; they broke their legs, they screamed, they tried to crawl somewhere aside.

The dark rust-brown cloud rapidly covered everybody.

Yangel failed to catch his hat. For an instant, he looked at the approaching swirls and then rushed towards the cloud. At that moment, a stronger explosion burst. The acid poured over everyone creeping along the concrete; it burnt Yangel's hands. People were coughing in whoops. Yangel dragged somebody on the concrete out of the cloud, trying to hold his own breath as long as he could. A man crawled towards him, raising his hand and declaring, "I am Gerchik, I am Gerchik . . ."

Security soldiers rushed forward from the checkpoint towards the cloud. They came round, stopped—nothing could be done to help. They screamed something, who knows what—simply screamed, like everybody else, with mouths wide open, in despair, out of helplessness before this sea of fire and smoke, as they watched people perish.

Military personnel and civilians jumped out of the bunker not far from the launchpad—they immediately became enshrouded in the cloud, coughed, choked, fell down in the cloud, crawled.

That day the fiery explosion took ninety-two lives.

Ishlinsky drove Stroganov away from the pad and thus saved his life. Kostya Luarsabov was saved by his own fast legs but had marks on his bald spot from acid drops. Yet, he had a whole life left. Yangel was saved by his hat. Only his hands were burnt by acid. Yangel had eleven years left.

Some years later, when I was leaving Dnepropetrovsk for Moscow, Luarsabov gave me a memento—a knife made by factory craftsmen out of cutting tools that cut metal like butter. I still keep it to remember a man who was born for the second time at the test range.

The test range was in a state of shock. Yangel was in shock. The KGB turned off the army high-frequency hotline between the test range and the outside world, just in case. Casualties were being carried from the launchpad to the hospital. The head of the test range was among them. The Central Committee representative, Stroganov, turned out to be senior in this situation.

He gave the order on communications: "Put me through to Khrushchev," he said.

In Moscow, they put him through to Frol Kozlov, then second secretary of the Central Committee in charge of defense affairs. Kozlov's reaction was rather single-minded.

"What's with Nedelin?" he asked.

"The marshal perished," Stroganov answered.

"Bring him here."

"So far, it's hard to identify him."

"What's left of him?"

"Charred char."

"Find Nedelin. . . ."

The search for Nedelin began. A metal bar for medals was found. Must be his. Suddenly, some glitter—it turned out to be one melted golden beam of the Star of the Hero of the Soviet Union. There was only one Hero of the Soviet Union among the victims.

At that time, only three people in the Dnepropetrovsk design bureau knew about the catastrophe and people's deaths in Baikonur: Vasily Budnik, Yangel's first deputy; the secretary of the party committee; and the chairman of the trade unions. A special closed army hotline from the design bureau to the test range was cut off. The phone operator on duty would simply reply to callers, "Communication with the test range is not available." Budnik got a phone call from Moscow about the accident. He kept information to himself, not knowing the details.

We designers continued to peacefully work in Dnepropetrovsk design bureau utterly uninformed. I was drawing the fuel-feeding system for a new heavy-rocket booster. The head of my group, Valentin Kovalchuk, came over to me.

"Listen," he said. "The central radio just announced the death of Marshal Nedelin, the commander-in-chief of the Strategic Rocket Forces, in an air accident. This was the announcement. But Nedelin is now at the test range, awaiting the launch. Has something happened there? What if the marshal died during the launch?"

"No, how could it be! We would know by now."

"But how would we? The line to the test range is closed—this is one more indicator. . . ."

In the evening, when I came home, my grandmother from Perm, my houseguest, returned from the city market.

"I heard at the market that your car factory had some big explosion and a lot of people died," she said.

That's the grapevine telegraph for you!

"Where did you get that?" I demanded.

"People at the market are talking."

"And how do they know?"

"This I don't know—how."

"And I work there, at that car factory—I would have learnt sooner than them."

I knew nothing, and at the market they already knew!

"All right, God be with them, maybe people are lying."

To this day, the channels carrying this early information remain a mystery to me. But people were not lying.

The next autumn morning crashed down on many families of missile-makers with blood-chilling news: a husband, son, or father had died. In our design bureau, the wives of those who died were brought to the office of the chief to get word of their loss. Afterward, they were walked out, supported by their elbows. They were put into cars with doctors and driven home.

The design bureau froze still. A question was whispered around: "But Yangel? Is Yangel alive?"

A government committee arrived at the test range to investigate the reasons for the catastrophe. Leonid Brezhnev was head of the

committee; Ustinov was deputy head—at that time he was chairman of the USSR Military-Industrial Commission of the Council of
Ministers.

Brezhnev summoned Stroganov and announced right off the bat,
"We understand that we are engaged in the most complex undertak-
ing. It's impossible to go without mistakes in such affairs. That's
why we are not going to carry out any investigation. We must get
rid of any technical shortcomings and continue the work. Announce
this to everybody."

"Leonid Ilyich, it will be better if you announce it," Stroganov
responded.

"Fine. Get the heads of the design bureau together."

The State Commission for Testing was gathered together. A young
woman, a designer from Kharkov, asked to say a word. She said
that she had made an error in the electric-circuit scheme, and, as
a result of this, instead of a weak testing current, a strong launching current had gone to the engine of the second stage during the
check-up of the chain of the launch pyrocharge. She said she was
ready to take any punishment.

But Brezhnev kept his word: there were no punishments or any
further KGB investigation of the reasons for the accident. This
designer was just sacked. Neither the chief designers and big bosses
in Moscow nor families of those who died demanded the blood of
the guilty ones. One thing was clear to everybody: thousands of
people are involved in the creation of a new and highly complicated
technology. Even the hard work of large numbers of people cannot
prevent mistakes; they simply need to be gradually captured and
eliminated, and all missile tests are carried out to this end. Officials
did try to make access to the launchpad regime tougher, but all in
vain. More people than necessary kept crowding the launchpad in
the future as well.

The Nedelin disaster was not the last catastrophe involving missiles. More than once people died in accidents. For politicians,
nuclear missiles were the virtual weaponry of the Cold War. But for
air-defense workers, these missiles were the actual weaponry of a
real, hot war, in front trenches where people perished.

CHAPTER 4

Baikonur Test Range

The chief designer of Yuzhnoye Design Bureau, Mikhail Yangel, said once in conversation with the man who would be the head of my sector there, Vladimir Kukushkin, "I need a trained manager for the R-16 project. The project is rolling on, no time for training. We need someone to plug in at once. Do you have a candidate in mind?"

Kukushkin said that yes, he had this kind of guy and gave Yangel my name. This was June 1961. At this time, I was living with my wife near the Dnepropetrovsk factory in the small log house of grand-dad Timofei and grandma Pasha. We had sent our little daughter to Omsk, to her grandmother, the previous summer. She was only six or seven months old at that time. My former colleague from the Omsk design bureau who had come over on a business trip took her with him. It was the beginning of a hot Ukrainian summer, so different from our Siberian summers in Omsk, even more so from the Urals summers of my youth in Perm. Here, the air was fragrant and people were dressed in minimal clothes. After work, we delightedly rushed to Komsomolsky Island's beach. I must have had too much swimming when I caught cold at the most unsuitable moment: the signing of the order to move me to the group of leading designers of the missile complex.

This group of leading designers was an elite division at the design bureau. There were three project areas at the bureau: heavy rockets (launch weight about two hundred tons), light rockets (about one hundred tons), and space vehicles. Each project area was headed by three leading designers of the missile complex, or, as they came to be called later, chief designers of missile complexes.[1] Each leading designer of a missile complex had his subordinates: rocket designers, land-equipment designers, and so on. There were not more than five or six people altogether working in each project area.

These leading designers were very active, cheerful, and resourceful people. Each of them, mostly, set his own prerogatives. The progress of the works within the big project, which involved five or six hundred enterprises, depended on these leaders. These leading designers were responsible for organization of the whole missile complex, from design decisions to delivery to the customer, which was the Ministry of Defense.

The scope of activity of a leading designer of a missile complex ranged from initial ideas and draft studies to decision making, with the right to sign documents at the launching pad on behalf of the chief designer of the design bureau. Such a leading designer was the main link between the design bureau and the Defense Department of the Central Committee, the committee of the Council of Ministers for military-industrial issues, the Ministry of Defense, and the designer's supervising ministry.

Inside the design bureau, the leading designer of a missile complex held carrot and stick. He reviewed the plans of design-bureau departments' work. He could criticize the performance of a subdivision, which would then lose its bonus, or he could sanction additional funds to reward the performance of a department, paying for it out of a fund that amounted to 2 percent of the project cost. These were very effective motivators.

When Kukushkin told me of his talk with Yangel about me, I first asked him, "Where could I get the flat sooner, with the leading designers or at the design-bureau department?"

"You'd be the only leading designer without a flat; they will give you one at the very first distribution."

That's exactly what happened, but in the meantime I still lived in the log house of granddad Timofei. I was quite ill, with a high fever—it jumped above forty degrees Celsius. I knew that something was happening at work and that this sickness had caught me at a bad time. I needed to quickly crawl out of it. To speed up the process, I swallowed antibiotics—tetracycline pills—which caused a strong reaction: all my mucous layer turned white. It was a mouth milk-fever, as sometimes happens to babies, on top of my cold. My mouth became impossible to open, and I could not eat or drink.

One day, in the midst of all this, Aleksei Polysayev, the leading designer of the R-16 missile complex, appeared in the doorway. He was a short man with an inflated sense of self-dignity: serious, self-important, and official.

"Vitaly Leonidovich," he intoned. "Yangel signed the order to appoint you to the group of leading designers for the R-16. Here is your business-trip paper; the flight to the test range is in the morning. We must prepare for the first launch of the missile after the catastrophe," he added, referring to the death of Marshal Mitrofan Nedelin in the terrible launch disaster. "Life goes on!"

"But I have a fever of over forty!" I mumbled with my cracked lips. "My tongue is swollen, I cannot talk, how can I fly?"

"I don't want to know about it. The order from the chief is for you to fly, not me. Obviously they want to give you a trial run on a tough assignment. Get packing! The whole crew of the expedition is taking off; there will be a load of work. The leading designer is in charge of the whole organization. After a break of nearly nine months, test operators have forgotten what a rocket looks like. And we all have to overcome the morale. You are going to be a new man there; it will be easier for you to adapt."

Galina pitied me, but she always took the job conscientiously: if this is required, then he'll have to go.

I got up early the next morning, with difficulty, and didn't even take my temperature. Walking on cotton feet and hungry—I couldn't put anything into my mouth —I dragged myself to the plant's checkpoint, with my suitcase; the bus was waiting there already. Fortunately, it was just a five-minute walk to the checkpoint. The people who were gathered there were really young, energetic guys—test operators—who all knew each other well. They dumped their backpacks and mesh bags. Jolly folks, they playfully poked fun and picked on each other. I was among this team for the first time. Friendly joking immediately tuned me into their wavelength and eased the tension of meeting a lot of new people embarking on a new endeavor.

In those days, we flew by Il-14. We filled two planes. In one corner, some passengers picked up at once with a game of cards, préférence. Others dozed off. Probably because of high fever, I felt nauseous. I used a tried and true remedy: I began to hum some songs to the music of the motors and hummed them all the way till we landed in Guryev, in present-day Kazakhstan, where we had a temporary stop. Everybody headed for the airport cafeteria, where drinks and red caviar sandwiches were waiting. I simply crawled down the stairway, never letting go of the handrail. After we reboarded, the atmosphere got noticeably livelier inside the plane. My companions started trying to "cure" me with vodka, but then, recognizing my inability to eat if I were to drink it, they just showed sympathy.

A monotonous grey and brown landscape stretched outside the aircraft window. Here was a new airport: sheds scattered around, houses of a town in the distance. For some reason, probably for secrecy, it had been given the name of Baikonur—the name of a distant village. In reality, it was the Djusaly railway station, near the small village of Tyura-Tam. In construction documents, this secret city on the barren steppe was called Object Taiga, which conjured images of a dense forest. Thus, for secrecy, a bald head can be called curly. Legendary constructor of the test range General Georgy Shubnikov had rushed the building of launching pads at the behest of his superiors. There were military specialists living in every direction. In 1956, despite prohibitions by superiors, about two hundred families came to town. A special mailbox that was attached to Shubnikov's car was filled with letters: houses had to be built fast; school had to open. On May 17, 1957, the first launch of Korolyov's rocket was made from launching pad No. 1. Regrettably, it failed. As the saying goes, the first pancake is a mess. The second launch, on October 4 of that year, was a success, and the launching pad went into operation. In 1961, when we arrived, Baikonur was only five years old.

The door to our cool aircraft opened, and I stepped onto the Baikonur airstrip. I leaned back: forceful heat hit me in the face, enhanced by the scent of herbs. Later, I experienced this many times in the sauna or a bath by pouring aromatic extracts on red-hot stones. The hot cement of the runway radiated haze; it all glittered in a smooth, lakelike mirage. The passport formalities were simple. Cars carried us to an apparent furnace. Sand to the left, sand to the right: How am I going to cope here, I wondered, where everything is unusual?

We drove for an hour and a half, past the left turn into the launch-pad from which Yuri Gagarin, who, as the first person in outer space, orbited the earth in April 1961, took off and on to the second launching pad, that of Korolyov. My escorts immediately explained everything to me, a novice. Here was launching pad No. 43—Yangel's pad. Next to it was launching pad No. 41, where the assembly-testing facility was located, as well as launching pad No. 42, sadly famous in connection with the death of Marshal Nedelin. It had a newly built launch installation.

The expedition was put up at hotels. I was given a room at the Lux Hotel, which was erected by the unskillful hands of soldiers and thus had cracked. Now and again, the crack in the light-pink facade of the Lux Hotel was sealed with grey cement, which didn't add to the charm of the hotel's crooked sign. But the accommodation had everything necessary to ordinary life, including a small cafeteria on the ground floor.

During the drive from the airfield and in the brief period of checking into the hotel, my high fever subsided, and the mouth milk-fever disappeared. For the first time in several days, I managed to get something in my mouth at the evening meal, first cautiously, then forcefully. What a health resort—I got cured in a few hours!

But of course it was not really a heath resort. I was a leader here, but I still had many questions: Whom should I be leading and whither? What were my duties? What were my powers?

There was a technical director of tests, Viktor Grachyov, Yangel's deputy for testing. There were test operators—specialists on each system—who had a specific task: to check the condition of their systems prior to a rocket's launch. They went through operations on a checklist to judge whether everything was in order for the rocket to be launched. I could not go to Grachyov and ask him, Is there anything for me to do here?

I decided to send up a trial balloon. I went to see the head of the expedition. This was an administrative job held for a long time by Andrei Gusev, the most gifted man in administration, especially in creating good relations among people. I gave him a simple task.

"Andrei," I proposed. "Give me the papers that need to be signed while there's free time for it."

"Oh!" answered Gusev. "The main papers here are requests for alcohol. They can be signed by either the leading designer or the technical director. Usually the leading designer does it."

"Is there alcohol here at least?"

"Listen to him! An expedition without alcohol! A railway tank car is standing at the ready—sixty tons—you could get washed away. Those willing to flush connection joints with alcohol will crawl to you. Don't indulge them too much, but don't disappoint them totally. Life here isn't home life. You'll understand if you stay here long enough. Both our folks and the military guys need relaxation. Also, a job needs to be done."

He brought me into a windowless room where a barrel stood in the center. Gusev patted it.

"Here she is," he said fondly, "Our old friend! We fill her up from the cistern and we serve here, upon written request."

Dispensing alcohol was the first challenge I faced. That same day, the pilgrims started coming.

"Twenty liters to wash contacts 'NN' at the hull floor of the first stage," one supplicant demanded.

I asked, "And how many contacts are there to wash?"

"I have four slots, approximately forty contacts each."

"And what will you wash them with?"

"A paintbrush."

"All twenty liters with a paintbrush?"

"One glass will be enough for a paintbrush."

"And where will the rest go?"

"Where will it go? We'll use it; it won't even be enough."

"Are there any standard dosages?"

"To soldiers, we'll give them a standard dosage."

"And what is the dosage?"

"Half a glass."

"Perhaps we can agree on two liters?"

"That would be better than nothing, but come on, write down five."

There were other, less acquiescent talks. Young lieutenants could be pushy and stubborn.

"Why did you come here?" one snarled. "You have to work with us, keep that in mind!"

"I will. And you keep in mind that you have to work with me. Deal?"

"No deal."

Alcohol was the currency of the launching pad in other more serious relationships, too. It was obtained with great ingenuity. For example, I needed to make a phone call to the design bureau on the army high-frequency hotline, a special channel for secret discussions. I gave the right number, but the operator on duty replied, "I cannot connect you: your name is not on the list of people with clearance for the HF hotline." What shall I do? Oh, Andrei Gusev knows everything, I thought to myself. I'll call him and explain, "So and so won't put me through!"

"All right, try to make a call one more time, in an hour," Gusev responded. "Meanwhile I'll find the operator and tell him to come over with his flask."

There were no problems with communications after that.

The resourcefulness of those looking for a drink knew no bounds. The military who worked at the assembly-testing facility were allocated alcohol in a twenty-liter laboratory glass bottle with a tightly lapped glass plug. They kept the bottle very secure. A paper strip was glued across the top of the plug with a top sergeant's signature written on it so that if somebody tore the paper to get at the alcohol the breach would be detected at once. But alcohol disappeared from the bottle anyway. When the time came to clean the contacts, no alcohol was available. The bottle was there, the lapped plug in its place, the paper strip with the signature not torn. It was clear what happened to the alcohol, but how did they get it without opening the plug? Soldiers were questioned. They looked confused, fearing that if they gave up the know-how they wouldn't be able to use it again.

"C'mon guys, tell us!" the top sergeant said, running out of arguments. "Talk. I give you the word of a gentleman, there will be no follow up."

"We all finished ten years of school . . ." one of them started.

"Very educated!" the top sergeant brightened.

"We've had enough education to figure out that the climate here is sharply continental: during the day, one meter away from the cement, it's up to eighty degrees Celsius, plus, but at night it's frighteningly cold. We measured it ourselves. We slightly shifted the lapped plug and flipped the bottleneck into a mug. More than half a mug got pressed out in one day: a law of nature for the benefit of mankind—a sufficient dosage. Thus, gradually, it all leaked out, and the tag didn't unglue."

"Academicians, alcodemicians! And I lost sleep because the bosses thought I drank the whole bottle and replaced the tag. I'll go make a report about the harm of education."

The secrecy of works at Baikonur was paramount, so launching pads were located at great distances from each other. This necessitated an extensive transportation and communication network. Thousands of kilometers of asphalted roads and railroads were constructed. At the beginning, the test range even did without a special hotline; to a certain degree the constructors found it more comfortable this way because they heard less scolding from distant bosses. Messages had to be sent from one railroad station to another. Later came the installation of thousands of kilometers of cable for specialized high-frequency communications.

The "capital" of the test range, launching pad No. 10 on the bank of the muddy and cold Syr Darya river, was known as Leninsk. A big town had been built right on the sand, with shops, kindergartens, and a beach along the river. There was a park—always crowded with young, fashionably dressed mothers with strollers—a big club, a library, a hotel and all the social challenges typical of territories cut off from the mainland.

Every morning the military compound in Leninsk swallowed up men through checkpoints marked with a red star. There, behind those gates, they performed something that was necessary for the life of the test range. They prepared rocket tests or they studied telemetry from previous tests. But the largest crowd of men hurried to the railroad station; from there, a rail motor trolley went to every launching pad. Every morning rail motor trolleys took military specialists around the launching pads. The rail motor trolley from Leninsk's launching pad No. 10 called on every launching pad twice a day: in the morning and in the evening. Unfolding at each launching pad was everything that Baikonur, this small state in the desert, a unique military emirate, was created for.

Another small part of this state's residents—most of them officers' wives—worked at kindergartens, schools, and shops. As a rule, their education level was excessively high for ordinary jobs, and the women personnel performed the work faultlessly. But these positions didn't remove the problem of desperate female unemployment. Every contract employee felt the hot breath of several candidates for her job. They feared the slightest dissatisfaction of their bosses because they could be simply sacked and replaced. (The trade unions here were accommodating.) "If only we had the same system around the whole Soviet Union!" I thought, overwhelmed by the unusual amiability of a food-store saleswoman. A woman in her position would not have behaved in such a friendly way elsewhere in this country.

One night, as I stood late at the Calculations Center in Leninsk, Sveta Oleinik of the design department said, "The car from the forty-third pad will not come for us any time soon, and it's the birthday of a lieutenant colonel from the Calculations Center; he invites us to celebrate a little. We could see how people live here."

I eagerly agreed. The house was a standard five-story building, with everything: a well-tuned piano, a guitar on the wall. We had a drink. We had a meal. If there is a guitar, it has to play its repertoire. The lieutenant colonel's wife picked it up. I listened with my mouth open. Even after all these years, I can still feel the surprise and pleasure from her beautiful voice, high professionalism, and fine understanding of the most tender notes. If only we had this talent around the whole country! Yet a talent such as this never went beyond the community club at pad No. 10.

One could get to pad No. 10 by car. Military commanders and chief representatives of the KGB at the test range had them. How much energy and funds had to be spent to pave those endless roads disappearing beyond the horizon, on sand: sand to the right, sand to the left. During the day, heat haze loomed over white-hot asphalt. There was nothing to catch the eye but a ground squirrel's figure occasionally appearing on a dune. Driving at nighttime was forbidding, too: a driver might start to slumber, and if a wheel slipped into soft sand, the car would start somersaulting. I had more than one chance to see the results of accidents on test-range roads here and can still picture it. A young soldier is behind the wheel. He was up early. He has the chronic sleep deprivation of a soldier. He is dressed in southern sackcloth smock, but he is still hot in his green uniform. Nobody else is on the road, in either direction. His eyes are puffed with slumber, his head wavers, the car slides into sand . . . dead bodies.

This is why we—test-range old-timers—were always vigilant: we constantly alerted the driver by talking or poking him. He would swivel his head madly, but bore no grudge. I remember one time when a driver suddenly hit the brakes abruptly, wheels screeching to a stop.

"I hit it! I hit it!" he exclaimed.

It turns out that a snake was crossing the road. Local drivers consider it the utmost accomplishment to skid on a snake and kill it. If you simply run it over, it then stays alive. Customs out here were so refined.

Many accidents injured people, too. Viktor Radutny, deputy chief designer of our friendly design bureau for engines, managed to get into car accidents at the test range more than a dozen times. At first, he would usually sit next to the driver and hit his head against the windshield in accidents. After yet another hospital recovery, he said,

"Enough." He began to sit in the back. Then his car was hit from the rear, and Radutny got seriously wounded.

Two cars once crashed head-on at our pad—one belonged to Chief Designer Yangel, the other to his deputy for testing, Grachyov. There were no passengers, but both cars were smashed to smithereens. The drivers—typical Russian lads, with their oddities and obstinacy— were hurt but still on their feet. At headquarters, they both stood silent like guerilla warriors during interrogation, so they had to be cross-examined one by one:

"What, didn't you see a car in front of you?" they were asked.

"Why, of course I saw it. I am not blind," each would respond.

"But why didn't you steer away?"

The replies that came were identical: "And why didn't he?"

Their irrational obstinacy made this a quintessentially Russian road accident.

While the military personnel of the test range lived a regular family life at the central pad, No. 10, the youth lodged around the group residences at the other working pads, and visitors on duty trips were put up in hotels. Days when we were on stand-by we had friendly feasts, barbeques to celebrate birthdays with picnics along the Syr Darya or by the artesian well.

The well was one of the sightseeing attractions of the test range. A pipe twenty centimeters in diameter and two meters high stuck out of the naked desert sand. A powerful spout squirted three to four meters up, the water falling back, fanlike, into a lake. This well had been drilled as a drinking place for antelopes, but crystal-clear water, a rich watermelon field along the shore, opportunity for a sobering dip—all made it quite a suitable place for a picnic. The main difficulty was finding this wonderful fountain amidst endless sand dunes. Test operator Sasha Bratsky damaged his spine when he dove in headfirst and hit the lake bottom. He spent half a year on a hospital bed. Nobody wanted to dive after that, but the appeal of the well as a picnic spot endured.

Once, three leading designers of missile complexes at the test range got together: Stanislav Us, leading designer for the R-36 heavy missile, and Leonid Kuchma, leading designer for space systems (who later became president of Ukraine), joined me, leading designer of the R-16, at pad No. 43. We decided to celebrate this important gathering with a picnic at the well. As we drove back from the well after midnight, our headlights spotted the ruts of jeeps crossing each other in different directions. This was because there were plenty of people eager to shoot saiga antelopes out of a racing car in the vastness of the test range, both military brass and industrialist-poachers. Refrigerators at the launching pad were stuffed with saiga carcasses for weeks. Sophisticated meals were cooked with the meat when people paid visits to each other for drinks and socializing.

And here we were driving in the dark. How does a driver find his way in the desert—by stars? I was sitting next to the driver. Sitting behind me was a jolly and ready-witted company. Stanislav Us, a communicative man and a big joker, in a jovial gesture, put his feet on my shoulders. I took a shoe off his foot and threw it out of the window. Us did not react. I took the second one off and threw it out. Us continued with his funny story. Then apparently his feet got cold in the wind. He pulled them back.

"Oh! And where are the shoes?" Us inquired.

"I threw them out of the window."

"How come, out of the window? Where shall we find them at night in the desert?"

"We probably won't find them. You'll have to go to the central pad barefooted to buy a new pair."

"But our State Commission sits in the morning! Am I to take the floor barefooted? Boys, let's look for them. Turn back!"

And where is "back" and "front" here, in this pitch-dark expanse? We traversed the sand through the night and found both shoes by morning.

Shoes figured in another funny trick I played on top officials visiting Baikonur Test Range. The birthday of a man whom I recall only by his last name, Colonel Kuslya, the senior military representative of the design bureau, was celebrated with a picnic on the Syr Darya at pad No. 43. Colonel Yuri Motovilov, representative of the Main

Directorate of Missile Troops Equipment, from Moscow, was present. He and Kuslya shared a room in the Lux Hotel.

Before bedtime, as was the pad's tradition, everybody went for a stroll along the concrete road. Night cold was pleasant after the day's heat. On the way back, Motovilov disappeared. Maybe he is paying somebody a visit, we supposed. Before going to bed, I went to check the hotel rooms to see whether everyone was back. Motovilov was nowhere to be seen! Kuslya was preparing to go to bed, polishing his shoes. The State Commission would meet the next morning, and he was going to speak there as the representative of the army quality control at the design bureau back in Dnepropetrovsk.

I asked Kuslya, "But where is Motovilov?"

"I don't know!"

Kuslya carefully put his shoes by his bed. He admired the polished luster.

"Then who knows?" I pressed. "What if he freezes in the desert? Maybe he felt bad?"

"Maybe bad. Motovilov is your pal, so you go and look for him."

A leading designer is responsible for everything. I went to search. I reached the road and circled the hotel. When I got back, Motovilov was already snoring like a motorcycle, and he had managed to polish his shoes to a shine, too. They stood on display, sparkling.

"Just you wait," I muttered.

I took both shoe pairs and put them into a freezer in their room and went to bed. My colleague Sasha Bratynsky came to me in the morning.

"Are you going to have breakfast?" he asked.

"I was looking for Motovilov half the night, running across the desert, while he slept soundly," I replied. "So I put both colonels' shoes into a freezer in their room."

"Wow. Let's play this card! I am going to call on the colonels."

He came back, smiling.

"I asked them a question: 'Do you know who left your shoes on the concrete road in front of the hotel?' They immediately rushed there to see!"

"And what did they say?"

"'No shoes there now,' those fellows said. 'They must have been our shoes! But we didn't come back barefooted, did we? How did they end up at the road?'"

The colonels didn't come to eat breakfast—they didn't dare show up in military uniform and house slippers. They didn't come to the meeting of the State Commission either. In the middle of the day, a hotel receptionist found me in the assembly-testing facility.

"A phone call for you," she said.

Motovilov.

"Vitaly, we somehow feel that you may have information about our shoes," he declared. "We mined the whole hotel, all the rooms. The receptionist didn't see any shoes."

"Did you look everywhere in your room?" I inquired.

"Everywhere, everywhere. We turned it all upside down."

"Maybe you didn't look everywhere after all."

Both colonels came to lunch, now in shoes. They clanked their fists together for us to hear the sound.

"When we put the shoes on, the cold froze us almost to the waistline!" they exclaimed.

Another, more sobering, episode involving Motovilov at the test range gave me food for thought. It was winter. Lots of snow had fallen. We had the day off, and there was bright sun—a good day for skiing.

Motovilov borrowed a hunting rifle from local officers, saying, "Perhaps I'll shoot a rabbit for dinner as we go; a lot of them graze around launching pads in winter."

We skied eight to ten kilometers away from launching pad No. 43, moving randomly. Suddenly, a jackrabbit hopped out of a burrow. It pricked up its ears and dashed away from us over a hill into the next hollow. We followed its tracks, which showed up clearly on the pure white snow. Motovilov was reluctant to shoot the rabbit. It was running from one burrow to another.

We climbed yet another hill. I can still picture what we saw there: a man lies in the hollow with fur-lined jacket, bunny boots, a helmet—a full set from the Pierre Cardin of the military industry. The man turned out to be alive; he was sleeping on the snow, huddled up. The daytime temperature was fifteen degrees below zero Celsius, but by evening, under a clear sky, it could go down to twenty or thirty degrees below zero Celsius. The lad would freeze in his sleep. He'll die, we thought to ourselves.

Of course, we granted forgiveness to the jackrabbit and let him go. The man was drunk as a skunk. But surely he is a hardy fellow, we supposed. He had marched through the snow in his dog-fur boots for ten kilometers. He had run out of energy and fallen asleep. If we hadn't appeared then, he would have been dead by the time anyone else came along. Who would think to search for him at this distance away from the launching pad? He is an easy pray for wild dogs, we fretted. They had already mauled more than one soldier here in the winter desert. That's why a special instruction banned people from going across the steppe alone. Hard as he tried to fight us off, we managed to put the man on his feet and force him towards the launching pad, visible at the horizon. He ran out of gas quickly, and we had to mercilessly slap him with ski sticks to make him move.

His legs held up until we got back. Steam began rising from his body as he sobered up a little. Along the way, he cursed us with his rudest vocabulary. He hardly understood that he had barely avoided death. He turned out to be an employee from a construction train that stood on the pad. We never even learned his name.

Now, let's think about this a little. Motovilov and I had spontaneously decided to go skiing. We came to the place with the jackrabbit. The rabbit led us right to the place where a man was lying and could have died. It brought us there to save him. The man survived. He is probably still alive, having produced children and grandchildren. And he never understood what happened.

How was it possible for all our paths to meet in the middle of a vast snowy expanse of desert? We, systems analysts by profession, could not even begin to calculate the number of zeros after the period—so small is the probability of all links in this chain of coincidences. Who was directing our skis? Who was directing the jackrabbit? Maybe fate played a role in this event. Or was it God?

Following the cruel Nedelin catastrophe, preparation for the first launch of the R-16 rocket was closely followed by both the Central Committee and the Council of Ministers, not to mention the Ministry of Defense. Dmitry Ustinov, its head, sent three ministers at once to monitor the progress on site: Leonid Smirnov, in charge of rocket equipment; Valery Kalmykov, radioelectronics; and Boris Butoma, rocket gyroscopes (in those days, gyroscopes were designed at shipyard enterprises).

Naturally, there was no ministerial kind of job for them at the launching pad. So, dressed in orange unpressed Chinese trousers and mesh football shirts, the ministers arrived at our launching pad, No. 43, from the central pad, No. 10, one morning. They energetically hopped out of their Volgas—Smirnov from one, Kalmykov and Butoma from another, shared one—and trotted to the assembly-testing facility.[2] With that, a great battle began.

Minister Smirnov (at that time the chairman of the State Committee for Defense Equipment) had to inform Ustinov daily about the progress of preparation for the rocket launch. At the same time, he had to prove his involvement in this business—three ministers can't just sit around doing nothing. Smirnov saw his role in pressing Grachyov to speed up the preparation for the launch. Kalmykov and Butoma mostly kept silent. Smirnov's queries and reproaches made Grachyov furious.

"Why are you rushing me?" Grachyov demanded. "You haven't seen enough accidents? They're the result of haste. I know what I need to do, and the military people know. No need to hasten people. Nobody sits idle; everyone knows his business and does his job. I don't have claims on people. I am not going to harass them."

Eventually, Grachyov managed to get rid of the unwelcome visitors. It all started when the ministers found Grachyov in a room with the army high-frequency-hotline gear. All three of them rushed in, sweaty, hot from a road trip and apparently another pep talk from Ustinov. Smirnov burst in first, as usual. The operator on duty quickly ran off. I stayed.

"Where is the schedule of work?" Smirnov, the main accuser, bellowed, hitting the table with his fist. "No schedule? What do you mean you don't need it? Then we are going to make one for you! Give me paper!"

The ministers sat down and wrote out a work schedule for the assembly-testing facility. Smirnov, the former director of the Yuzhmash plant in Dnepropetrovsk, had a general idea about the nature of the work on the rocket. So he listed the necessary tasks:

- check-up of control system—completed: time, date
- check-up of hermeticity—completed: time, date

And so on; there were five or six lines in all. Then he gave the paper to Grachyov, who, again, exploded.

"I told you," Grachyov burst out. "I am not going to work to schedules! This is not boots-cobbling, for hell's sake! With this schedule we'll only provoke people into rushing. They must do their complex jobs, not mind the schedule."

"You don't understand the situation, comrade Grachyov!" Smirnov, who was not used to such firm resistance, retorted. "The preparation for the launch is being watched by the leadership. If you don't want to listen to what you are told, I am going to remove you!"

"Go ahead and remove me! I am not going to discard people!"

"I will remove you! Where is the leading designer?" Smirnov turned to me and said, "So, you are the leading designer? Here is a schedule for work at the assembly-testing facility. Go and organize!"

I was quite willing to disappear from this unpleasant battlefield, so I grabbed the paper, gave it to the typist, and went down the stairs into the cool hall of the assembly-testing facility. A slightly phlegmatic captain named Perevozchikov and the head of the assembly-testing facility, Major Aleksandr Matrenin, stared at me.

Matrenin smiled a little and said, "They say the situation among the superiors got glowing hot?"

"Yes, they are about to have a fistfight. Here is the schedule of work at the assembly-testing facility for you; the ministers drew it up. They ordered us to fulfill it and report on it. Please!"

I handed the paper over. Matrenin hid his hands behind his back; Perevozchikov did, too. Matrenin wanted to say something but only shook his head at first.

Then, he erupted, "Vitaly, go rub your ass clean with this schedule! Ministers instructing me on how to work at the assembly-testing
facility—what do they understand about it? Ministers!"

Later, Matrenin became a general and the deputy minister of
general machinery building. I sometimes reminded him of this scene
at the assembly-testing facility, and he just laughed it off.

Grachyov immediately called Yangel in Dnepropetrovsk and told
him that Smirnov had no confidence in him; thus, Yangel's presence was required. Yangel flew in the next day, quickly came to
understand the situation, and called Ustinov to reassure him in his
usual diplomatic manner with soothing words along these lines:
"Everything is going according to the plan. All the specialists are in
place. And there is no need to permanently keep such respectable
and busy people as the three ministers at the launching pad. They
will be of considerably better use in Moscow." Apparently, after this
talk, Ustinov called Smirnov at launching pad No. 10 and recalled
the trio. The ministers left, never to show up at pad No. 43 again.
Our work continued at its own pace.

Marshal Kirill Moskalenko, chief inspector of the Ministry of
Defense, often visited the test range, first as commander-in-chief
of the Strategic Rocket Forces and later as the top inspector. He was
another intrepid character who figured in our work at Baikonur.

The marshal was actively interested in all the events at the test
range and watched over the provision of every amenity, even meals
for soldiers and officers. His inspections were useful in snapping our
people into action. The test-range folklore describes this case. Once,
prior to Marshal Moskalenko's arrival, they noticed that the grass
in front of the HQ hadn't been watered for a long time, and it had
withered and turned yellow. They froze in fear: the marshal's rage
was imminent. They urgently drove a compressor over and painted
the yellow grass with a cheerful green. Later, they referred to it as
a rare kind of grass called Canadian lawn.

But I remember Marshal Moskalenko for a different reason. This
was another launch of the R-16 rocket, which had already sent many
people into coffins, including Nedelin. Moskalenko, who came to
the pad that day, decided to watch the launch from close proximity,

not through a periscope from inside the bunker. Usually, before a launch, all the residents of the pad were driven out to the steppe. Test managers—both civilian and military—stayed in the bunker during a launch. Moskalenko decided to watch this launch from a pavilion on a hill, about two hundred meters away from the launchpad. This pavilion, along with a covered caponier near it and a not very deep trench, had been built earlier for launch observation. However, since the Nedelin accident of 1960, the pavilion had remained empty during rocket launches, now considered too close to the launchpad. But no one dared to say no to the marshal, and he took a position in the pavilion together with five or six officers. Gas masks, field glasses, and mineral water were delivered. The breeze blew favorably from the pavilion towards the launchpad. The weather was sunny and excellent.

As the leading designer, I was delegated to the pavilion to answer any possible questions of the marshal. There was no need to do this, but I was very pleased about it: at last, my long-standing desire came true to watch the rocket launch from a close distance. Another one of our test operators tagged along with me: Anton Bondarenko. He dealt with various buggies for transportation of rockets, and he had been disabled from childhood, when both his legs were cut off by a streetcar. Anton carried his massive body on crutches. He stumbled along to the pavilion and apologized for being late. He had had to catch a ride since walking on crutches doesn't get one very far.

The launching pad's diesel power station—insurance against a power shortage— monotonously hummed at the same pitch. Already, hardly any people could be seen around the pad. Colonel Aleksandr Kurushin, the chief of launching pad No. 43, announced his famous line to the whole place, "I am Kurushin. I go into the bunker!"

As was the tradition, Tchaikovsky's Piano Concerto No. 1 started to play. This signaled the thirty-minute warning. Rockets and Tchaikovsky: What's the connection? And why Tchaikovsky and not Skryabin's Prometheus, for example? Or Bach's organ music? Or some other composer's? And why is music needed here at all? I took a long time to consider various combinations. I played the music in my head.

What is a rocket on a launchpad for a human? It's a whole kaleidoscope of sights, emotions, hopes, frustrations, and wild happiness. The rocket is a concentrated essence of concerns and the labor of tens of thousands of people. In some ways, it is their common idol. It is alive and capricious, unpredictable and dangerous. It can murder or reward, with a will of its own. And everybody waits to see how this idol will choose to act.

And what does the launchpad look like prior to a rocket launch? It is a completely empty place, with no people. Tension can be felt in the air. Powerful spotlights hang from masts, like at a stadium. There is the girded platform of the launch table in the center of the pad. Brightly lit, the white obelisk of the rocket points up against the sky that's black at night or blue during the day. In keeping with the white color of the rocket, each of its slaves handles the idol with tenderness and love, wearing white coats and white gloves. This was the only way they worked at the assembly workshop. Once the rocket goes into serial production and becomes tamed, like a seemingly docile lion, it will be allowed to dress in green, which is the more typical color of its masters.

At the entrance to the launchpad, where the fueled rocket was standing, each friend of the rocket was given a heat-resistant steel bracelet with a stamped number. Many people had been simply incinerated at the previous catastrophe, and it had been difficult to identify them. But now—God forbid!—each one's ashes would already be numbered with the bracelet.

Everyone behaved differently before the launch. The brain cannot easily contain so many emotions at once. Some exhibited heightened chattiness and exaltation, with unnecessary gestures. Others developed an inner shivering, a vibration. When the first sounds of the piano were heard at the launchpad, people somehow shook off part of this heavy load of emotions. This music was chosen by a very smart man.

I can relive the moment still. In the pavilion, we are listening to Tchaikovsky. A public address system reaches there. The five-minute warning is announced. Moments later, Tchaikovsky's music is muted. An announcement comes over the loudspeaker: "Pull down!"

"Aye, aye, pull down," the telemetrists respond.

This means that telemetric recording tape would be slightly pulled aside so that there would be a few seconds of emptiness marking the start of the launching process; they are now ready to pull their recording tapes, starting with a new tape.

"Key to launch!" the announcer barks again.

"Ayes, key to launch."

"Launch!"

"Ayes, launch!"

A muffled burst. A rusty cloud rushes away from the rocket. Talk inside the pavilion stops. We wait tensely for the sharp nose of the rocket to appear from out of the cloud.

"Do it, do it!" we cry.

Bending down with tension, we seem to be trying to pull the rocket up by hand.

"Come, baby, come!" we plead.

But there's no rocket! No rocket! It's not there! One second after another ticks by as we try to comprehend what is happening. No! The rocket's engines are on—did it fail to lift itself up? What is holding it? Fingers clutch the pavilion's handrails.

"Go, darlin', go!" we cheer vainly.

The wind blows the launch cloud away a bit, and it becomes more transparent. One can see very well: the rocket has left the launchpad and is moving just above the ground. Only two out of three engines of the rocket's first stage have started. The effort of two engines is insufficient for a flight, but the rocket's control system is keeping it vertical with the finesse of a balance master. Thus, vertically, with strain, sobbing, blowing away the sand with the engines' stream, the rocket floats just above the ground, slightly wagging its hips—the protruding cowling of the control thrusters. To this day, it is unforgettable.

"Oh! The rocket is dancing a death tango! Put the music on!" we exclaim.

The public address loudspeaker is silent. The rocket flies, but where? Operators haven't sorted it out yet, confused by the telemetric data. Finally, they find the formula, and a stumbling voice cuts through the loudspeaker:

"The rocket is in movement!"

But the rocket is moving towards the pavilion! Towards us! Not too fast, but it is getting closer.

"Aaaaah!" we cry.

There is motion in the pavilion. The marshal's entourage is the first to rush out of the pavilion and head haphazardly down the path. Their general direction, however, is away from the rocket. I dash to the nearest shelter, jumping over the trench. Somebody dashes behind me. I don't see who it is, but the back of Anton Bondarenko's white shirt—he managed to find a place for himself face down in a narrow trench—is marked with a dirty shoe print. Somebody ran across Anton's back, over the trench. Later, Anton cursed it very funnily, remembering the moment with humor.

I dive into an open door and immediately jostle my way close to the thick reinforced glass and lean on it with both hands: Where is the rocket? I just have time to take in the awful scene: blowing sand up with a fiery stream and a muffled roar, the rocket stumbles against a pile of metal railing around the launchpad with its bottom part and falls on its side.

The explosion rocks us. A brown cloud, spinning fast, rolls up and sideways but does not reach the pavilion. The wind helps direct it away. Besides, the pavilion was built by experts. I look carefully where the explosion cloud moved, away from us. Good! Luck is with us! All this unfolds in a few seconds (reading about it takes much longer).

I crawl out. Silence. Anton, stuck in the trench, is already unbending himself.

"I can do it myself!" he protests. "Some reptile stepped—"

"Stepped on what?"

On his back! I help him get out. He tries to explain something but stutters more than usual with fret.

"Who stepped . . . ?" he sputters.

I just wave my hand: it was time to get back to the pavilion to see what was going on there. A grand performance is on: the last act, the finale of a tragicomedy!

It turned out that during all these events Marshal Moskalenko didn't move from his place. True, I could not imagine this marshal could run from any threat, even if his life depended on it. He was strict, always pompous and slow, sparing his movements, over sixty years old, until recently the commander-in-chief of the Strategic Rocket Forces and today the chief inspector of the Ministry of Defense. Surely Moskalenko saw the rocket moving towards him perfectly well. Maybe a thought such as this crossed his mind: This rocket is a killer of marshals and commanders-in-chief of the Strategic Rocket Forces; it will kill a second marshal, this time myself. Not bad for history!

But who knows what Moskalenko thought at that moment. The marshal did not run. He remained standing still, left alone in the pavilion. Thank God, fate kept the marshal safe when the rocket didn't reach the pavilion. Interesting—did he believe in God?

And now, half turning, Moskalenko silently looked from above at runaway officers who had deserted him; they were returning to the pavilion shrunk to dwarf size and staring at the ground.

The marshal didn't say a word of reproach to them. He said nothing about this case to managers of the test range. I don't think he shared it with anybody at the Ministry of Defense lest the information reach the Central Committee. They might have disapproved, saying, "Why did you go there?" They might have considered his bravery to be vain bravado. They have their own rules at the Central Committee after all. But the marshal's silence spoke louder than words.

CHAPTER 5

The R-16, R-36, and Other Missile Projects

The R-16 missile, NATO designation SS-7, the first in the series of heavy strategic missiles, experienced many failures. A fatal curse seemed to be upon it. Almost a third of this missile's launches had accidents. It was history's first heavy strategic combat missile of intercontinental range. It weighed about 150 tons; it took almost three tank cars of nitric acid and dimethylhydrazine, the most carcinogenic fuel. The missile could fly for eleven to twelve thousand kilometers and was capable of carrying a big hydrogen bomb. It was a truly diabolic weapon of mass destruction. The missile was born from a fierce feud among design schools. Today, it would be called a scientific-technical war between military-industrial clans. There were victims here, and winners. The victims were banished as pensioners or moved to lower posts; the winners got prizes in the form of Gold Stars, academic titles, seats in the Supreme Soviet— positions in the hierarchy.[1]

At the end of the 1950s, several alternative ways of delivering a heavy hydrogen bomb to a target at an intercontinental distance were examined. The major strategic sites in the United States, at that time the enemy of the Soviet Union, were easier to reach via the North Pole. The Soviet Union's aviation system did not ensure such delivery because of their vulnerability. For at that time, the United States was already creating the North American Aerospace Defense (NORAD) system, a powerful air-defense barrier in the northern direction.

Yangel's R-16 missile was examined along with the draft of a cruise missile by Chelomei's design bureau and the R-9A missile by Korolyov. The cruise missile possessed all the drawbacks in vulnerability that are typical of a plane. The R-9A missile required complex means to maintain it in constant combat readiness at launch position. Liquid oxygen that was boiling inside this missile's tanks at regular temperature had to be continually captured, liquefied, and returned to the missile's tanks. But the R-16 had the launch weight of about 150 tons and possessed manifold strategic abilities. It weighed just above ten tons without fuel; it was filled up with fuel at the start position, during the mounting. Building of the R-16 missile conclusively established Yangel's thread in the direction of liquid-fuel components on combat missiles: hydrazine and nitric tetroxides instead of cryogenic components which boiled in missiles' tanks at regular temperature. Work on the R-9A cryogenic-propellant combat missile at Korolyov's design bureau was closed down for good as a result.

Already in the first years following the Caribbean crisis, approaches to strategic nuclear weapons noticeably changed. The Caribbean incident shifted us from a relatively simple decision process to deliver a nuclear strike, as the Americans had done to Hiroshima and Nagasaki, into a more complicated, political decision process. As missile technologists, we had frequent spontaneous chats about nuclear engagement, saying that nuclear missiles won't be put to use, that it's a suicidal process for an aggressor, that retaliation is inevitable. But somehow there was no place for these conceptual-level talks at the design bureau—people there were immersed in engineering problems. Complex strategic matters were mostly the prerogative of Yangel and his closest deputies, who were ten to fifteen years older than we were and had accumulated the intellectual depth required for these conversations. This combination of mature leadership at the top of the design bureau with the high abilities of young guys who implemented the ideas was giving, as always, the most productive results in technology.

Chief designers don't invent everything by themselves. A lot depends on the level of their selected team. Rocket technology was a fairly new activity, and it was more successful among the young teams—young guys who were not engaged with design traditions and preselected paths and directions from a different era and different people. These young guys were not yet trepidatious in front of superiors and were quick to turn the new technologies that came their way into specific commodities.

Yangel had a youthful design bureau: the average age of employees of Yuzhnoye Design Bureau in 1963 was twenty-six—when one's whole life is still ahead! To the credit of the design-bureau heads—Mikhail Yangel and Vasily Budnik—it must be said that they had a keen ear for young thought; they did not try to crush it, and this brought high dividends.

Certainly, this was not the case at every design bureau. Korolyov derived and publicized the dialectical formula of relationship between a chief and his subordinate designers. He told his designers something of this kind once: "You must do this. If you don't do it, I'll sack you. If you do do it, I'll get a reward!"

There were worse variants also. A leading designer of Korolyov's design bureau told me that, during a conference, as Korolyov paced behind the chairs of participants, he grabbed a T square and hit this leading designer—he was guilty of something—on the head. The T square broke, and Korolyov threw it on the table and left. The next day the leading designer was transferred to another design bureau with a slight promotion.

I once had a chance to take part in a big conference before academician Nikolai Pilyugin, who was considered a patriarch of control systems in rocket and space technology. About a hundred people came, sitting packed at the long table. Pilyugin and the commander-in-chief of the Strategic Rocket Forces stood at the head of the table.

"Go ahead, make the report!" Pilyugin said, nodding to his specialists.

At the beginning of the report, all was calm.

But suddenly, Pilyugin slammed the table with his palm and commanded, "Stop! Stop! Let me say a word!"

And he began speaking on the issue at hand. I watched people's faces on both sides of the table grow longer as they realized: the chief is saying something incorrect! Finally, Pilyugin noticed this facial ballet, too.

"What? Am I going off track?" he demanded.

"Yes! Yes!" everybody confirmed, nodding vigorously, "Off track, Nikolai Alekseyevich, off track!"

"Even if I am going off track, we will do it the way I say!" Pilyugin insisted.

Yangel managed things differently. Of course, one can suppose that he was not aware of all the details of designers' work on specific matters, but still, at the design-bureau conferences for high-ranking guests from Moscow, the reports were always made either by leading designers or project-makers, if the project was still nascent. These young people handled all the questions from the audience. Yangel did not interrupt anybody; he only made himself prominent at the final stage of the conference as he summarized the results. He could disagree with something in the report of a leading designer or a project-maker, but he did not disrespect it; for the guests, he would present his objections as debatable ideas, as other possible options. When discussing it with the leading designer afterwards, he did not press his authority but simply asked for explanations as to why it was said this way and not another way. Besides, by standing aside while the frontline youth made their reports, Yangel could observe the reaction of visiting superiors from the wings and adjust his subsequent actions accordingly. I think this was an ideal method of brainstorming. It did not waste time and effort on persuading the boss or smoothing internal frictions. This kind of liberated mentality always yielded good results. Later, I constantly tried to implement this approach in my work at the Central Committee.

Yuzhnoye Design Bureau and its chief designer Yangel, successfully showed that the R-16 intercontinental ballistic missile with a launch weight of about 150 tons was simpler and cheaper than a cruise missile of 40 tons by designer Vladimir Chelomei and his Reutovo design bureau of machinery building. Chelomei's project was closed down. Besides, the project of launching a cruise missile did not satisfy the requirements for this type of weapon to penetrate the enemy's air-defense system. Regrettably, the technical argument that began between Yangel and Chelomei at this stage later grew into an open rivalry between these too prominent specialists, even a personal enmity.

Yangel knew that the R-16 missile meant more than just a victory over the cruise missile project; it was also a confirmation of his correct decision to use liquid fuel that under regular temperatures could remain for ten years or longer in the tanks of combat missiles on duty. Yangel was right, but this had to be proved to many people.

Parallel with the R-16, Korolyov's design bureau was creating combat missiles RT-1 and R-9. Academician Vladimir Chelomei's design bureau was offering a strategic intercontinental cruise missile to be called Burya. It was a battle of elephants at Thermopylae! Four concepts collided. It really was a battle at the cross-roads: Which road should rocket technology take?

In the United States in that period, the development of solid-fuel missiles was quickly accelerating. The Americans had a big advantage; they were one up on producing complex technology in many ways. For one thing, the quality in our country was worse. In American conditions, quality control was imposed with more vigor than in our system. The risk of losing their jobs because of poor outcomes was the last thing to concern our workers because they knew if somebody tried to kick them out that person would pay a price! The high quality of chemical products and technologies allowed the U.S. specialists to combine the main energy ingredients—oxygen and hydrogen—in a solid rocket fuel better. Similarly, the Americans had construction materials of higher quality and durability which were resistant to the flow of exhaust products.

Despite the challenges in our country, with great effort, Korolyov managed to create an experimental sample of a solid-fuel combat missile, the RT-1. Single copies of this missile were tested at the Kapustin Yar test range near Volgograd. I made a special trip to the test range for a clandestine study of this missile (competing designers carefully kept their secrets from each other). The missile's simplified exterior and lack of customary pipelines and numerous other elements typical for a liquid-fuel missile surprised me.

At the same time, Korolyov proceeded with a second line of combat missiles, R-9, fueled by liquid oxygen, to replace the R-7 missiles. A combat missile, which must be ready for launch at any time, ought to be provided with nonstop replenishment of liquid oxygen inside a closed loop. This complicated the whole launch process. But Korolyov obstinately stuck to his guns. R-9 launches mostly ended up in accidents. These were grandiose night fireworks, when dozens of tons of fuel merged in one explosion at the missile's crash. It wasn't even an explosion but some powerful expiration, the heavy breathing out of the earth, which would suddenly tremble under our feet.

Korolyov's RT-1 missile could carry only a small warhead. The R-9 missile answered the requirements of permanent combat readiness only with the use of complex energy-consuming launchpad devices. In the end, both were closed down on a specious pretext: it was necessary to concentrate the efforts of the design bureau on preserving the Soviet Union's advanced position in space research.

Academician Chelomei proposed an interesting alternative missile. My impression from personal meetings with him is that he was an extraordinary and engaged man. He had little concern for the difficulties accompanying his work; he was continuously lured by original solutions and was in a hurry to get a final result. He went most profoundly into the problem that was vital for rocket technology: the problem of vibrations. But for some reason, vibrations were the curse for Chelomei's missiles. Indeed, he was a cobbler without shoes.

Chelomei directed the experience of his design bureau in aviation technology and combat cruise missiles towards the large project of an intercontinental cruise missile with a straight-flow jet engine. But nobody in the world made such an engine. It demanded the resolution of many scientific-technical issues and large amounts of money, and this work could stretch on for years, while the missile was needed immediately.

Separately, Yangel proposed the R-16 intercontinental missile to carry a large hydrogen-bomb warhead. It's no big deal if a combat missile is an enormous size. Well, the R-16 weighs about 150 tons with fuel—but this is "still-standing" weight, which a missile carries at the beginning of combat duty only. As it starts moving, it loses the weight while the fuel is being used. An intercontinental missile can stand filled up for ten years and longer. This was more or less the reasoning of Yangel and the Dnepropetrovsk designers, and they turned out to be right. There are missiles of this design bureau which stood for twenty years, filled up with fuel components—nitric tetroxide and asymmetric dimethylhydrazine. And they could have kept standing on, if they had not been taken down by the axe of disarmament.

The R-16 became the leading missile of the whole line of heavy missiles from our design bureau in Dnepropetrovsk. This line became the foundation of the Soviet defense might, the foundation for the whole range of rocket boosters. But it was plagued by misfortunes.

One missile went down within sight of our launching pad. This was a night launch, with all the effect of fireworks. During the start of the engines, at the beginning of the launch, in the bright light of spotlights, some gas emission was seen on the side of a small hatch, at the bottom part of the missile. For some, it seemed to be an obvious fact; others argued that it was only an illusion. I also saw this outflow of either gas or flame as I intently watched the start of the launch through field glasses.

Most likely, the specialists decided, there had been some small explosion in the engines compartment. For this reason, the engines of the first stage functioned abnormally, and the missile began to swing. The second stage broke off the first stage and went down, overtaking the first stage. And the first stage, with one of its three engines shut down, got free from the payload and the upper stage and made death loops in the starry night.

Stars here in the desert sky each look like they're the size of a fist, but our handmade star was larger. It crisscrossed the black sky in zig-zags. The roar of the engines was heard in waves. There was little understanding where the devil would carry it, so the people on the ground, just in case, ran in all directions, against all logic. The place of the missile crash was later located, and, in the morning, plans were quickly made for analysis and a search for remnant parts.

Yangel's first deputy, Vasily Budnik, was the chief manager at this test. Budnik was a most extraordinary man. He was one of the founding fathers of the design bureau, a precise, pragmatic, strict, and even harsh manager. His orders were carried out at running speed. Yangel used to send Budnik to the test range at the end of the year, when it was time to present a report about successfully completed annual test plans. In accordance with the Russian style, all this business was done in the last days of the year, right up to December 31. When a plane roared above the roof of the design bureau in the middle of the Ukrainian winter's thick fogs—no land can be seen from the first floor—everybody knew: only Budnik would dare fly home in this weather. And it was him indeed. This happened many times. And in any weather, any time of day or night, Vera Ivanovna, his wife, waited for him at the airfield. This was a time when Budnik was rounding up winter launches from the annual plan, and the missile had decided to fall! In the morning, they found the little white hatch that fell off the missile, which meant that there had been an explosion in the aft section after all.

"Who saw the emission of gas in the hatch? What did you see?" Budnik asked of those gathered at a conference meeting in the morning. "Who saw the little hatch fly? We must collect all the bits for analysis. We will drive there in several groups and walk in a line at five-meter intervals. The suspect is the tank of launch fuel and the gas generator; they must be found, definitely."

The crater at the place of the first-stage crash still smoked, like a vent of a lazy volcano. Half a kilometer away a second crater smoked, left by the upper stage, but it was of little interest to us. We spread out into a chain as we got closer. Budnik walked next to me. And—such luck!—I strolled into that very tank, a deformed pipe a meter long.

"Here! The leading designer is lucky! Ace cards dealt to him," Budnik exclaimed. "Now, he has to find the gas generator. We'll have to dig into this hole; the remains of the engines lie in the crater, hence the gas generator must be there too."

The gas generator was the size of an ordinary three-liter jar, but with superthick walls. Naturally, it had burrowed into the sand like a bullet. We drove back to the pad together with Valentin Derkach, engines test operator, to prepare for the excavation. Compartmental gas masks were scarce; they were preserved for superiors in bunkers at launches. We found ordinary gas masks. We dressed in boots, helmets, jackets. We drove again to the smoking crater. The soldier behind the wheel watched preparations with curiosity.

"Are you going to climb inside there? Into the acid? Such a cool job," he commented.

We took turns going to the bottom of the crater, the other one assisting from the top. We shoveled the acid bog for five to ten minutes at a time. Sweat covered the glass of the gas masks. Acid bit at our teeth. My shovel ground against something hard—but there were no stones here. What's this, I remember wondering, and I feel as if I were there now.

I am short of breath. Up! Up! I silently plead, deprived of speech by the gas mask.

"Give me your hand! Leave that shovel there!" Derkach calls.

Done. The gas mask is torn off. What air! So good!

"Something creaks under my shovel there," I report. "If its big, we'll have to hook it to a jeep with a steel cable, we won't be able to pull it out like this."

"First let's try digging around it," Derkach proposed.

And thus, we dug sand one at a time, acid slurping under our boots. We dug for half a day. The soldier driver had time to make a pretty belt out of the colorful wires of the rocket. Finally we pulled out two gas generators. One of them was among the suspects but perfectly undamaged.

"All for naught, damn it!" Derkach cursed, wiping his sweat and throwing the handkerchief into the pit. "Got to check telemetry and the tank. Let's go!"

Boots, jacket, pants, and helmet had to be thrown away; they had simply corroded in acid fumes. I was wearing a grey woolen pullover under the jacket; it changed its color to orange. Shirt, undershirt, and underpants were marred with dirty, rusty blotches. I wonder what blotches marred my lungs?

Meanwhile, the design bureau in Dnepropetrovsk proceeded with its other projects. The heavy missile R-16 paved the way for the whole direction of heavy missiles, but with difficulty. R-16 launches and their analysis required a lot of time, but the experience gained was put to work straightaway. A project was started for a new missile of the R-16 type, with all shortcomings of the R-16 to be taken into account. Its registration index was set by the military as 8K66. Mikhail Galas was this missile's leading designer. A highly dynamic expert, by that time he already had the title of Hero of Socialist Labor for his work as the R-14 missile's leading designer.

The 8K66 was made almost in one breath. First, examples of the missile were manufactured for flight-testing in a short time. They just waited for an instruction from Moscow to send the missile to the test range. But instead of this instruction, an order from the minister to curb work on this project arrived. The reason given was that the new missile was not a serious step forward in comparison with the R-16. This decision was probably fair.

Also during this period, the design bureau worked on an assignment researching silo launch, a new kind of deployment of strategic missiles. By that time, a silo had already been tried on the intermediate-range missiles R-12 and R-14, the Dvina and Chusovaya projects. The project for the R-16 silo launch was called Sheksna. The Sheksna silo was built a little bit further away from launching pad No. 43, and a new concrete road was paved out to it. This road became a favorite place to stroll after dinner, after the exhausting heat had passed, when it was possible to comprehend what had been accomplished during the day. We talked shop as we walked or simply chatted about daily life problems.

The silo was built in an open-cut method. First, a gigantic foundation pit was dug out. Next, an iron and concrete structure ten stories high resembling a vertically placed submarine was erected inside the pit, which was then covered with sand. Requirements of full autonomy dictated that this "sub" had to be equipped with numerous systems. For example, one of the silo's levels contained two excellent diesel power stations. These stations were in constant readiness to function in seconds—their diesel engines didn't even need a warm-up; they stood hot all the time. Later, when in the mid-1970s the stations were simply destroyed as the silos were modernized—no other use for them was found—their warm, glossy, grey-lacquered hulls always stood before my eyes in mute reproach.

At the same time, following the 8K66 missile, the Yuzhnoye Design Bureau was engaged in analysis studies of the conceptually new R-36 heavy-rocket complex, whose missile's launch mass was almost sixty tons heavier than the R-16's. Upon return from the test range from a regular launch one day, I was pleasantly surprised when my colleagues greeted me with congratulations.

"Vitaly, you are lucky! You just finished one project and already got assigned to the next one," they said.

"Which next one?" I asked.

Aleksei Polysayev, my direct boss, explained, saying, "Commissar" (for some reason this was his nickname for me), "I sold you to Yangel for the thirty-sixth device. You will work independently, and all that's left to do here is to divide bonuses and medals; this I will finish myself somehow." He stood up, shook my hand, and pompously added, "Congratulations! A big ship deserves a big cruise; I am certain that you will cope."

I went to see the project designers. Erik Kashanov, then head of design work, who always spoke in machine-gun bursts, started saying something almost incomprehensible, in his usual rat-a-tat-tat, about people mushrooming like rockets or rockets mushrooming like people.

"Congratulations, congratulations! Join in!" he fired.

"But nobody asked me," I blurted, trying to stick in a word.

"See it this way: you have the credibility of the higher-ups' trust— they assigned you to this project!" Kashanov raised his finger, triggering a final round, "Go for it; fathom it deeply and broadly."

Having toiled on the R-16 project, I now intensively studied to reeducate myself in missile specifics in this period. The duties of a leading designer had no clear boundaries. Even formal guidelines for the leading designer position were nonexistent at the design bureau back then. Many times we tried to draft such a document, making use of accumulated experience, but it was repeatedly turned down by Yangel's deputies, who saw it as an encroachment on their prerogatives. We were arguing that the power of deputies was exercised vertically, but those silos required connecting people from different disciplines—and this is the function of the leading designer. Eventually, Yangel, who was schooled through the mill of being a leading designer, ended up writing the guidelines himself, but even these were only an approximate framework. In reality, each leading designer took upon himself as much of the job as he could.

I got a big notebook and wrote down what I had to do, either now or later. Once a task was completed, I marked it with a circle and looked at what was next. There were many hundreds of items. This was mostly routine managing while I saw myself as a designer. A designer ought to generate ideas and organize implementation of his and other people's ideas—this is his major task.

Certainly, there were plenty of ideas. I looked at many design solutions with the eye of an aircraft maker. Having worked at a serial-production aviation factory, where a lot of processes relevant to flight had already become customary, it was surprising to me that, for example, they did not have pattern-cutting technology for large aluminum plates in Dnepropetrovsk. They had almost no aircraft makers at this missile factory. The personnel at the plant had initially been hired to produce automobiles, and they had even made a small test fleet of little dump trucks, which still ran around the plant in my days. Similarly, nobody at the plant had given serious thought to the repair and service of elaborate missile complexes yet—such gaps were simply patched with a business trip by a designer or test operator of the design bureau. This was still possible while there were only several tens of missiles around, but the production of hundreds of missiles was coming next.

Thanks to old friendship ties with the Omsk Civil Aviation Plant, I ordered documentation on pattern cutting, as well as on operations and maintenance of a plant. Surely the people at my new factory could have done all this without me—perhaps they would have eventually—but at that time they did not know these documents existed. Major conflicts occurred with project designers. They had become a particular kind of group, with its own way of doing things.

Ideas from the "outside," including those of the leading designer of the missile complex, were treated as alien. But I was hardly deterred by this.

The first thing that had surprised me about the R-16 missile was the arrangement of control instruments. Equipment was stuffed around in different corners of the control compartment. Each instrument maker built his unit in its own shell and stretched wires from it to another unit. All units were connected into a joint system in the missile-assembly workshop through rather bulky, complex, and not very reliable plug-and-socket connectors. Connectors were washed with alcohol before plugging. Many times I stuck my head into the control compartment of a missile under assembly and bumped into a familiar still-life picture: a green metal can with alcohol stands in the compartment with a slice of rye bread and a cucumber—the classic snack to go with a drink—lying next to it. I would take my head out and see a silent question in the several pairs of eyes around me: How did he guess where our stash was?

Testing of the control system at the missile-assembly workshop and at the range clearly showed that the more connectors there were the less reliable the system would be. And this was true even when a lead organization was assigned to each missile's control system. Why not merge the whole assortment of instruments into a joint hermetic encasement, fill it with inertia gas, test it at the instruments' factory, and, only after this, mount it on a missile as a joint module? The initial R-16 design team—Valentin Avtonomov and Arnold Nazarenko—did not turn the idea down at once, but they expressed doubts.

"Who is going to take on himself the additional burden of assembling all these instruments at his place? Besides, some electric imitator of a missile will be required to test this superblock at the instruments' plant!" they protested.

"Sure," I parried, "it's more convenient to off-load it all to the missile plant and then keep a crowd of instrument monitors there to catch their 'bugs,' instead of connecting and testing it at home!"

My final argument was a blow under the belt.

"Perhaps that catastrophe at the test range wouldn't have happened because of an error in the control system," I poked, "if the whole scheme had been tested on a missile simulator."

The project designers proved to be right: the design bureau of Vladimir Sergeyev, in the Ukrainian town of Kharkov, refused to even hear about such a plan of operation.

Some years later, I repeated an attempt to merge the control system into a joint module, for a different missile, the solid-fueled RT-21. During a talk at which Yangel was drafting concepts, he picked up on the idea with enthusiasm.

"Go ahead," he assented. "Let's press forward with it, although it is going to be hard to push through. Write an appendix to the technical requirement."

The appendix was received by the Kharkov men as expected, with bayonets. But Yangel already had a firm faith in the advantage of this scheme. He also was aware of Sergeyev's healthy conservatism, which even a minister found hard to break, although sometimes Sergei Afanasyev, the minister of general machine-building, could bring Sergeyev to tears.

When I managed to speak with officials at the design bureau in Kharkov about it, they responded, "Don't even hope, the granddad won't agree: an array is easier to off-load, and the whole module—who's going to take the fall for everybody!"

I went to Yangel and told him of Kharkov's position.

"Well," said Yangel, considering the situation. "There is no way we can heave-ho the granddad. We toiled along with Rudyak for a long time over the silo's design and had to sack him in the end. Is Sergeyev next?"

"There must be some solution," I rejoined.

"There is a solution, but it's rather radical—to take Pilyugin's control system for RT-21, instead of Sergeyev's. But it has gone too far already."

Yangel paced behind my back for a long while, lost in thought. He had no previous experience of so openly switching horses in midstream. He was searching for his own arguments.

"I will have to explain this offensive step to Sergeyev, prove it to the minister, explain myself at the Military-Industrial Commission of the Council of Ministers," he said at last. "It will reach Dima.[2] Grechko? No, I won't have to explain it to him—he is ill disposed toward this missile."

In the early 1960s, it was obvious even to young designers at the design bureau that the Soviet Union was never going to be the first to make a nuclear strike. We knew that only a guaranteed retaliatory strike from the Soviet Union could provide effective deterrence. For this reason, our nuclear-missile forces had to be able to withstand a first strike. Only one measure existed at that time to accomplish this: hide the missiles underground.

Together with the design bureau of general machinery building, which dealt with missile-launching facilities, the first experimental silos were built at the Kapustin Yar test range near Volgograd: project Dvina for R-12 missiles and project Chusovaya for R-14 missiles. A missile was loaded into a silo, but it stood empty, without fuel. Under increased combat readiness, the fueling was done by special fuel transporters. During the launch of a missile, the superthick lid of the silo would be opened, and the missile would start freely, rising out of a thick cloud of rust-brown gases, which would come out of the gap between the silo's wall and the missile.

Silo launches generated many problems. A silo and its protective lid had a wide diameter, which made the missile more vulnerable to a nuclear strike. Also, an unforeseen problem emerged: the acoustic effect of the silo on the missile. The sound of the working engines of a missile would bounce off the silo walls and create powerful vibrations that would wobble the missile while it moved inside the silo.

The R-12 missile did not always fly successfully. Almost every third missile launched fell down onto the steppes of the Volgograd region. Works immediately started at Dnepropetrovsk design bureau, and at Korolyov's design bureau before it was closed down, to use this former combat missile for launches of space devices. For this purpose, a second stage was designed for this formerly single-staged missile. As a space booster, it was designated the 11K63.

Thereupon, a whole space division was established at Yuzhnoye Design Bureau to produce scientific and military satellites. Those satellites under five hundred kilograms were called "Dnepropetrovsky satellites," or simply DS. Vladimir Kovtunenko, the former head of the planning office at the design bureau, became the head of this space division. A war veteran, he was significantly older than we were yet made sure to always be among young people. One could have an argument with him as a peer, row with him until one's voice became hoarse, with no negative consequences. We, the young men, just loved that man. I managed to stay on a friendly footing with him until his final days.

The encouragement of creativity and the direct involvement of the chief designer set the course for pioneering directions both at the design bureau and the factory. Yangel saw this creativity as an integral part of making missiles. Some of them have never been surpassed. The silo-based mortar launcher—a kind of cannon with a payload of over two hundred tons in a number of cases, such as in the case of the R-36 (SS-18)—was built. The missile was lifted by a solid-fuel charge located in the bottom of the silo. Then the first-stage engines were fired once it cleared the silo. We were nearly ten years ahead of the Americans on this technique. It entailed overcoming some serious difficulties: a whole branch of gas dynamics had to be established, and unique test stands had to be built. Project engineers wavered in the face of these challenges. Their hesitancy infuriated Yangel. His will to succeed spurred them on in the end, however, and a pioneering missile complex was the result. This is a little known part of the history of missile technology, and few people know about Yangel's fury over it.

A unique rail-based strategic-missile complex was created at Yuzhnoye, too, with the solid-fuel RT-23 (SS-24) missile. The tasks involved in bringing on line a vast network of railroad tracks which could be used for moving the launch complex were worked out. The Americans never dared to build such a complex, although they worked on it until the mid-1960s.

CHAPTER 6

Two Profiles: Chief Designers Mikhail Yangel and Viktor Petrovich Makeyev

Mikhail Yangel's life, starting from the end of the 1950s, was filled with creativity. The design bureau which he lead got firmly on its feet around this time, winning a good reputation by successfully creating a series of missiles. Young people gathered together at the design bureau; the chief crackled with ideas. The ideas did not always fit the job framework, so some new divisions appeared in materials science, dynamics, and space. At one point, they even experimented with dynamic thrusters based on Norman Dean's ideas. The Strategic Rocket Forces, created in 1960, were equipped mostly with Dnepropetrovsk-made R-12 and R-14 intermediate-range missile complexes and R-16 intercontinental missiles. The capabilities of Yangel's design bureau were ahead of military needs. However, the R-16 catastrophe that killed Marshal Nedelin, in which Yangel survived by force of a miracle, laid its hot brand on him. This he wore to the end of his life. Yangel could only shake off his feelings of guilt for other people's deaths with the help of wine.

I met Yangel for the first time in 1960 in the first days of my work at Yuzhnoye Design Bureau. New faces were all around me. I noticed that some man who was unknown to me said good morning at the entrance as I arrived for the day. I thought that perhaps he was confusing me with somebody else.

I asked my new colleagues, "Who is he? He says hello to me but I don't know him."

I was told, "Katayev, you are amazing! It's Yangel! He always says hello first."

Chief Designer Yangel encouraged forthrightness and unconventional ideas. He often started group brainstorming with a request to say everything that sprang to mind. "Any nonsense will do; we shall sort it out together, extract the rational seeds," he would say. He pulled young designers to his level: he didn't build a wall between himself and his subordinates; he didn't kick anybody out of his office when he spoke with higher managers. This episode is characteristic. He once said to me in conversation, "What, am I smarter than others here? There are people who are way more intelligent than me, but the circumstances turned out this way that I am in charge here."

The chief designer liked to design out loud: he paced behind our backs and spoke about the way he saw the solution to a problem. For his counterparts, he would choose people who would not be shy about contradicting him, who would put forward their alternative and even get stubborn in a good, argumentative way. Apparently, he had a good sense of a person's creative potential, and this sharpened the outlines of his ideas. He particularly liked it when subordinates didn't play up to him but rather picked apart his ideas. He didn't take offense; he would say something like, "You're right! I am sorry; it's not you who is talking nonsense, it's me talking nonsense. I now see it myself."

The major achievement of Yangel was the great collective of thinkers, project engineers, and designers he created. There were failures from time to time, but there was always confidence, which gave him wings. Yangel attempted to break psychological barriers in communicating with the upper leadership so as not to deprive the design bureau of its due share of attention. He did his best to defend employees. Sometimes he sighed, "They are going to scold again in Moscow; I'll have to go myself." He trusted people to the end. He realized that we were engaged in a highly complex enterprise, where mistakes are possible due to this complexity, not because of negligence.

In all his actions, Yangel was guided not by personal advantage, nor by advantage for his bureau, but by the interests of the state. Even when it was clear that rivals in competing projects were openly bluffing, Yangel demanded an honest approach; he did not allow fraud.

Yangel supported the decisions of his team even when those decisions contradicted his own. For example, one day the party committee of the design bureau was discussing the behavior of one of the department heads who had acted arrogantly and rudely, doing the bureau harm by aggravating relations with allied organizations and with his colleagues. Yangel stood up and said that he would not consent to removal of such a valuable specialist from his post. Everybody spoke and raised their hands in favor of removal. Forgetting that they had their hands in the air, everybody watched to see what the chief would do. Yangel took a handkerchief out, wiped the sweat off his forehead—and then raised his hand! How many managers are capable of doing such a thing?

No one can rise to the top without creating some friction, but Chief Designer Yangel's great professional rivals spurred him on to new heights. Chief Designer Vladimir Chelomei's design bureau specialized in cruise missiles. These were excellent devices. The Soviet Union was ahead of the whole planet on this type of weaponry. These missiles served both the coastal defense and the navy. There were interesting projects developing these missiles to use them to strike submarines.

But Nikita Khrushchev made his own kind of decision. Naturally, Khrushchev did not read the publications of foreign military theoreticians, particularly those with a fascist doctrine. Hence, he was unaware of the bankrupt claims of the Italian general Giulio Douhet, presented in his *Command of the Air* in the 1920s. Douhet insisted that aviation was capable of deciding the outcome of a war. Khrushchev made up his mind that missiles could achieve that today. "Long live the missiles! No need to spend money on aviation and the navy!"—this was his doctrine. Thus, the period of liquidation of vessels and aviation projects began, which included reorienting a number of aviation design bureaus towards missile technology projects. Chelomei's design bureau was changed, too. He was handed the design bureau of aviation designer Vladimir Myasishchev and a large factory. This became another large missile structure parallel to Yangel's design bureau.

Upon orders from the top, a large group of specialists from Chelomei's bureau arrived in Dnepropetrovsk. They were the most experienced aviation designers. Because of their poor knowledge of rocket specifics, they sometimes asked rather silly questions in the opinion of the Dnepropetrovsk youth, but they were digging very deep and were highly qualified.

The first results were reported to Yangel: "Chelomei's men have scooped up all our best and potentially promising solutions!"

Yangel flared out, "But this is our competitor! Why are you opening up so much? Give them general information only."

Yangel's position became instantly known to Khrushchev in Moscow, so the process of mastering missile technology at Chelomei's design bureau went on with direct participation of Nikita Khrushchev's son Sergei. A personal order from the senior Khrushchev followed: hand over all the necessary documentation to Sergei Khrushchev. Apparently, the personal dislike between Nikita Khrushchev and Yangel originated from this episode.

But the missiles were a serious trump card in political confrontation. The Caribbean crisis was one of the first episodes to demonstrate this. The R-12 missiles, which were produced in Dnepropetrovsk, were transported to Cuba. Telemetric missiles available at Kapustin Yar test range were hastily reequipped: telemetric equipment was removed from them and replaced with nuclear warheads. Although the specialists of the design bureau and of the manufacturing plant both participated in this work, a repair job is still a repair job, particularly under test-range conditions. Nikita Khrushchev requested a personal guarantee from Yangel on the performance of the missiles. Yangel gave it. The missiles fulfilled their first major political action.

Yangel failed to show up at a demonstration of missile technology to the country's leadership at the Baikonur test range, which was attended by Nikita Khrushchev. Yangel's first deputy, Budnik, represented the design bureau.

To watch missile launches, General Secretary Khrushchev and guests arrived at a bunker that had been specially built in the desert for spectators. Tables laden with the most exquisite fruit, samovars, and candy were set out for the dignitaries. The guests were voraciously swallowing up watermelons and juicy amber-colored melons. The minute the guests left, we managed to lay our hands on that fruit. Never again would I taste melons that melt in the mouth quite like that or pears so ripe that the seeds luminated through their transparent pulp.

Khrushchev, in the bunker, up to his ears in a healthy slice of watermelon, looked at the people around him.

"And where is that Yankel?" he asked.

"Not Yankel—Yangel, Nikita Sergeyevich. He is slightly unwell. His first deputy Budnik is here."

"Unwell . . . unwell. I know his sicknesses. His sickness is a bottle of vodka and a herring's tail—that's all his sickness. And what are we waiting for exactly?"

"We are waiting for your order, Nikita Sergeyevich."

Khrushchev tore himself away from munching on the watermelon and, as if he were conducting an orchestra with the rind, he pointed it upwards towards the launchpads seen in the distance and nodded his head.

"You there, launch it, launch it! What are you waiting for?" he demanded.

To speed up the launch time, the missiles already stood with prewired launch-readiness codes, which were paused on standby at the last step. So, following the waft of Khrushchev's watermelon rind, several places at the horizon thundered, and several strategic missiles climbed up one by one like slim needles.

The observation bunker for the supreme command had been sited with great ingenuity: if several lines were drawn on the map through the missiles' launch facilities, these lines would cross at the point where the observation bunker was situated. The launch facility from which the missile was going to be launched was oriented toward the top brass in the observation bunker, but they were not told that aligned precisely behind it, like a kebab on a skewer, several other launchpads were placed. If something happened to a missile at the first launchpad, a launch would be immediately triggered from the next launchpad aligned behind it, but this could not be visually determined from the bunker. From the bunker, everything would appear to be in order.

Naturally, Yangel was told about Khrushchev's humiliating public demarche at the test range. Yangel got alarmed—Khrushchev's disrespect was bad for the design bureau. He could pull any stunt; there were already examples of his slapping design bureaus down with one scrape of the pen. Yangel even began discussing among a tight circle of colleagues whether he should invite Sergei Khrushchev to be his deputy; one or two expletives may have laced his words.

By some uncharted route, these discourses of Yangel reached Marshal Andrei Grechko, the defense minister. He gave Yangel the epithet of an opportunist. Well-wishers made sure that Yangel learnt of the marshal's words. Yangel immediately dialed Grechko's number using the army hotline and announced that he was not an opportunist and had never sold his conscience to anybody. And he slammed the phone down. This gesture spoilt the personal relationship between Yangel and Marshal Grechko for a long time. As was typical of his nature, Grechko transferred the feeling of enmity onto business, on the work of Yangel's design bureau.

I even had an argument about the very last document of Yangel's career—a memorandum to the Central Committee regarding the creation of the rail-mobile missile complex. True to form, Yangel let me argue my own case. I managed to overcome Yangel's opposition, and he signed the text that I had prepared. After this, I drove to the academician Pilyugin, who started to offer the same criticism as Yangel. I dug in my heels again. Pilyugin phoned Yangel.

"Mikha-el," he said, slightly changing the name's pronunciation, "your lad is arguing, he disagrees."

Yangel could be heard replying, "I suggested the same thing to him, and he argued with me, too. Tell him that he cannot out-argue the two of us now—he should make the change."

I made the change.

Yangel was tactful in his contacts to the very end. I once had to square off with him on an urgent issue when Yangel, very sick at this point, was headed home for the day. I must have driven him mad: he dropped a profane word. I turned around and walked out. When Yangel got home, he called me on the phone and apologized. How many examples like this can anyone count?

The last time I met with Mikhail Yangel was in Moscow during the last full day of his life on October 24, 1971. He had finally returned to Moscow, for good. Heart attacks and a life of constant traveling on assignments had worn him out. In 1954, when Yangel was offered the directorship of Yuzhnoye Design Bureau, he assured his wife that Dnepropetrovsk would be a temporary event. It wouldn't last long, he thought: he would just train a suitable replacement and come back. His wife stayed behind in Moscow. But his enthrallment by rocket science and the level of responsibility he held, coupled with a desire to salve his ongoing feelings of guilt for the tragic demise of dozens on October 24, 1960, did not allow Yangel to quit from an up and running enterprise.

When Yangel had come to the design bureau in Dnepropetrovsk for the last time, he had asked me to sort out his personal archive, together with the head of the secrecy department. There were several suitcases of notebooks, project diaries, loose notes, and documents. Spreading it all on the floor of Yangel's house, on the slope of a ravine of a Komsomolsky park, I was trying to imagine whether Yangel would ever make use of these priceless materials.

Yangel showed up and asked, "How is it going?"

"Well, I am considering whether these materials will be handy for your secret memoir," I replied.

"Don't write me off entirely. We'll work again! I'll be coming over to you more than once."

"No, you won't. Once you've decided to gather up all your booklets and notebooks, it means you have seriously decided to move to Moscow."

"Perhaps you are right. But I will continue to work."

On that visit to Moscow, when I was already prepared to go to the railway station for my return to Dnepropetrovsk, I decided to call on him one more time before I left town. "It would be right to congratulate the chief on his birthday, since it's tomorrow—sixty years," I thought to myself. I had frequently called on him before, when I had to sign some papers, and I would collect his membership fees along the way—Yangel continued his party membership at Yuzhnoye Design Bureau.

"O-o-o! Hello, hello," he cooed. "Well, come in! Ma'am," he added, turning to his wife, "bring the watermelon, Leading Designer has come over! Fire away, tell of your comings and goings."

We ate the watermelon together; I told him a little about the job and wished him good health.

"I see that you are holding your suitcase already," the old chief designer observed. "Thanks for passing by. Ma'am, come over here, Leading Designer is leaving! I am not inviting you to stay. Pity, but I don't orchestrate my own birthday. Pass on a big hello to the guys; I hope I will be in the bureau again, more than once. They say that I was appointed as advisor somewhere, but it doesn't change anything. Bye!"

He waved once.

The next day I showed up at the bureau in Dnepropetrovsk in the middle of the day. It seemed strangely quiet there. This was an unusual silence for my room. My guys were sitting and reacted oddly to my greetings: they stared at me without speaking. The glass door swung sharply, and Yuri Andrianov rushed in.

"Did you come from Moscow?" he burst out.

"Yes. Why?" I answered.

"Prepare to go back—Yangel died!"

"How . . . died? I met with him last night. Everything was all right. He asked me to pass on his hello to you."

"He died one hour ago, right at the ceremony. In the hall of the collegium. The door opened, Chelomei walked in with flowers to say congratulations. Yangel saw him and sank to the floor. That's all. They couldn't do anything. . . . We are taking a train."

The period of close work with Mikhail Yangel was a grand school of life for all of us. I would like to wrap up with a brief excursion into philosophy. The figure of Yangel concentrated, if I can put it this way, all the dialectics of the tragedy of capital *P* Personality in our time: the country was fortunate that Yangel was the creator of her nuclear shield. He made us secure. Yet, at the same time, the country was unfortunate that such a bright and powerful mind for statesmanship was not called upon for a job of an even bigger scale and was limited only to the nuclear shield. But isn't untapped potential the last tragedy of a Personality?

In 1976, after my transfer to Moscow, to the Central Committee, I came across Viktor Petrovich Makeyev. Unhurried in his deeds and words, Makeyev was dealing with the difficult, multifaceted problem of building sea-based strategic missiles that were unrivaled in the Soviet Union. In the 1950s, in the period of establishing the country's new line of defense—nuclear weapons for a retaliatory strike—he had been the only one of the few leading missile specialists of Korolyov's design bureau who agreed to leave Moscow and head a new, secret design bureau in the Urals outback, in the city of Miass in the Chelyabinsk region.

When Makeyev took over, offshoots of the design bureau soon sprouted all over, not in Miass itself, which was dominated by a factory making dump trucks, but away from the town in an undeveloped area. A major settlement grew quickly there, a whole city—a design-bureau compound. In the meantime, along with the Miass design bureau and also in the Urals outback, in the city of Zlatoust, the production of strategic sea-launched missiles was set up, and a similar plant was simultaneously built in Krasnoyarsk. Machinery building in Miass accelerated rapidly. The first D-2 missiles of the 1950s, mounted on Soviet diesel submarines, added confidence to the Soviet political leadership, even if these weapons did not make a measurable change in the potential for a retaliatory strike. Makeyev started all this from nothing.

Municipal services required no less attention than missiles. There were big and small construction sites, where buildings housing daycare, kindergarten, and cultural activities were built for the specialists. Chief designer Makeyev took great pride not only in creating missiles and unique test stands, among which, for example, there was a vertical stand for testing in zero gravity, but also in making things for everyday needs, such as, for example, a gigantic wooden barrel for pickling cabbage. This barrel would be presented to me as a world-class achievement which did not make it into the Guinness book of records only due to the high secrecy of this Soviet missile site.

One day, Viktor Makeyev was receiving Grechko at his design bureau in Miass. There was plenty for the minister to see at this center for strategic sea-based missile weapons, the only one of its kind in the country. Makeyev met the minister at Chelyabinsk airport. They took a military helicopter to the design bureau's machinery building compound, which was located slightly further away from Miass. All of Makeyev's inventory was well on display from the air: a recreation facility, a pioneers' camp, rig-testing equipment, the chemical production plant where missiles were filled up with liquid fuel.[1] Next, the design bureau appeared on the mountain slope.

The minister pointed down with his finger and ordered the pilot, "Major, land here!"

"Ay, comrade Marshal, I will now make a turn against the wind," the pilot replied.

"I order you to land! Land now!"

"I cannot go against procedure, comrade Marshal, there are mountains here and a forest. I must land strictly against the wind."

"And I order you: land!"

"Comrade Marshal, I am responsible for your safety, so, I am sorry, I cannot comply with your order."

"Take his shoulder straps off. Dismiss him from the army! Write it down!" Grechko commanded, nodding to his aide.

Everybody on board fell awkwardly silent.

The helicopter landed according to all rules. The minister was received at the design bureau with interesting reports and with an open table—the usual hospitality. At the time of the party's departure, Makeyev approached the marshal, who was pleased with their reception.

"Andrei Antonovich, I have one favor to ask of you," Makeyev begged. "Please don't punish the helicopter pilot. He did everything as would be appropriate, complying with the procedures for safe flying; he cared for your safety."

"Good." The minister nodded and poked his finger at his aide saying, "I cancel it."

Following my first meeting with Makeyev in 1976, I came to be on friendly terms with him, although he had initially received me with caution, as if I were just one more inspecting bureaucrat. Thanks to that meeting with him, I finally grasped the wisdom of my new bosses at the Central Committee Defense Department in throwing me, a specialist in ground-based strategic-missile complexes, into supervising sea-based missile systems.

When I had expressed bewilderment, Stroganov, the head of my sector, had replied, "Pass your experience on! There is a lot for them to learn from Dnepropetrovsk! And Evgeny Krasnov will continue to handle it all at the Central Committee office. After he retires, we'll pick a man from Miass and let him pass Makeyev's experience on."

And that's how it would turn out: Makeyev's deputy for projects planning, Yuri Grigoryev, came to work at the Central Committee department. A very high-class specialist, he indeed began to deal with problems of ground-based missiles, including all the issues of the Dnepropetrovsk scientific-industrial enterprise, which was known as Yuzhnoye.

By the time I met him, Makeyev's design bureau already had four missile complexes as assets, including those on nuclear submarines. Makeyev had been awarded two stars as a Hero of Socialist Labor; he was a member of the Central Committee and a deputy of the Supreme Soviet, academician of the USSR Academy of Sciences, laureate of the Lenin Prize and the USSR State Prize. Hence, he would sport all the most honorary regalia of the Soviet Union that traditionally accompanied a successful career as a defense branch executive.

And Makeyev was the single absolute executive head of one branch of the strategic triad—the sea-borne one. This situation was at odds with the defense policy carried out by his boss Dmitry Ustinov, a military-industrial-complex old-timer who always sought to duplicate work and create at least a slight hint of competition. There were multiple factories producing sea-based missiles, so duplication of the product was accomplished at once, but it didn't work the same way with the design bureau. Attempts were made to create a replica design bureau in Leningrad—Arsenal Design Bureau, named after Mikhail Vasilevich Frunze. But there was only one Makeyev, in Miass. The Leningrad design bureau's work culminated in manufacturing just one D-11 missile on solid fuel. This missile failed to find a place for itself among the sea-based strategic arms of the Soviet retaliatory strike force, so it was settled on one submarine, supposedly to offer experience with using sea-based solid-fuel missiles but mostly to avoid giving offense, and to lend moral support, to the Arsenal bureau.

Specialists at Miass design bureau were not deprived of attention. New directions stimulated the writing of new theses. The authorities used awards in an attempt to somehow compensate specialists of the design bureau for their lifestyle in the Urals outback, which was a far cry from life in the capital; besides, their achievements deserved encouragement. Small anniversary celebrations at the design bureau's Palace of Culture simply sparkled with awards.

Come to think of it, everything was available there in the Urals to live, work, and enjoy the result—overwhelming respect. But the chief designer was unhappy. Makeyev lived in Miass without a family. His wife refused to go to the middle of nowhere with him. His children stayed behind in Moscow with her. Makeyev worked hard at the design bureau. He would have worked around the clock had he been surrounded by people living like bachelors as he was. But all around him was normal family life, and the chief had to return to his empty flat.

The only entertainment on weekends was going fishing, and fishing Russian-style is a well-known phenomenon: fill a glass and drink it down. The driver usually provided the refreshments. Companions were overabundant for this pastime: all fishermen of the design bureau had cars, and fishing places were widely known. With these constant fishing outings and basket picnics in the open air, Makeyev decided to go deeper into the Urals wilderness and even bought a motorcycle to this end. When Minister Afanasyev learnt about it, he panicked.

"Victor will drive himself into a coffin on this motorbike! We know all about this kind of fishing! Where were your eyes, why didn't you inform me!" he said to his assistants.

Afanasyev personally called Makeyev and asked him to get rid of the motorcycle.

Despite such recreations, Makeyev seemed weighed down. Relations with his wife did not improve. A passionate woman, she suffered without a husband. In her rare visits to Miass, she made scenes of jealous accusation; she had a banal jealousy of her husband's secretary. On some occasions, she complained to me on the phone that they were turning her husband into an alcoholic in Miass. She did not hide the fact that she would like to divorce the academician and have a simple, normal man. These could be found, but they disappeared as soon as they heard that she was the wife of a secreted academician.

One day, Makeyev came to Moscow with scratches all over his hands and face.

Jokesters did not miss a chance to ask, "Oh, Viktor Petrovich, did a big pike come your way when you were fishing? She left scratch marks all over you."

Makeyev sneered, "Right, it was a big pike, if by pike you mean my wife!"

To my satisfaction, our relations quickly became well tuned. Makeyev liked a good joke. He was self-deprecating and never missed a chance to criticize bureaucrats in an unspiteful way. He saw me not as a Central Committee employee but as an experienced specialist and stressed this more than once. This is why our relations were so productive. Not only was I able to introduce some Dnepropetrovsk experience, but I managed to do what I had failed to do in my native design bureau.

Here is what happened. Makeyev was very swift in reacting to a small diagram of per unit weight-efficiency of warheads of the strategic missiles of the Soviet Union and United States in which I compared the quality of the American and Soviet warheads. Our warheads came across as being much worse: they were heavier despite the equal yield of the nuclear charge. Hence, we had to make more powerful and bulkier missiles to carry them. Together with Makeyev, I discussed the reasons for our backwardness and possible ways of improving our warheads. Makeyev himself undertook a search for new technologies and managed to find the key technology.

He called me on the army hotline and said, "Vitaly Leonidovich, remember our talk about warheads? It appears that there is a method for moving ahead. Interesting work in the field of metallurgy is in progress. Those guys need only a little bit of help. We'll help them— we'll be customers for their product. Talk to the director of the works. Interesting prospects may open up. Oskar Akramovich Kaibyshev is going to give you a call, do receive him for a talk."

Kaibyshev showed up at my office at the Central Committee soon thereafter. A deeply provincial scientist, profoundly immersed in science, he talked about metals like a gardener does about plants. If his achievement in processing metal in superplasticity could be applied, the advantage would be obvious. We could make warheads that were not so heavy. We arranged a technical training at the Central Committee Defense Department. Kaibyshev held himself with confidence under the hail of questions from the wise men of the Department; he spoke convincingly. I discussed Kaibyshev's work with Moscow specialists. They confirmed the potential of the technology but alleged that this technology had been known for a long time and that they had invented it.

I called the first secretary of the oblast committee of Bashkortostan, in the city of Ufa, Midkhat Shakirov, and told him about the importance of developing a new technology in his republic, explaining how its application may contribute to the development of Soviet strategic weaponry. I recommended that they should invite Kaibyshev for a talk. Shakirov did just that. He interviewed Kaibyshev in detail, going into the essence of the matter and giving it serious consideration. To strengthen his opportunities to promote the new technology, Kaibyshev was elected a deputy of the Supreme Soviet. A decision was taken to build a new scientific-technical base in Ufa—an institute and experimental production facility.

We managed to get the defense ministries who were interested in the new technology involved and to invest a small share of funds. As a result, a modern scientific and experimental base was built—a problem-solving institute called the Institute for Metals Superplasticity Problems. The institute counts among its accomplishments numerous scientific discoveries and thousands of patents; it is recognized around the world. Kaibyshev became a cochairman of an international committee for problem solving—this is practically the only example of such high recognition of the institute's performance. During the collapse of the Soviet Union—a nearly total collapse of the country's industry—this institute would be one of only a few that preserved its personnel, its scientific potential, and global leadership in creating materials with superior characteristics.

Another example of significant innovation at Makeyev's design bureau was its work on warheads that could be independently targeted during the final leg of their trajectory. This boosted the precision of sea-based strategic missiles. Although the line of independently targeted warheads was eventually closed down, the foundation for making them for sea-based missiles was laid.

Makeyev was quick at assimilating new ideas; he moved forward from one missile to the next. Designers of the submarines carrying the missiles, including Sergei Kovalyov and Igor Spassky from the Leningrad design bureau called Rubin, were like-minded associates.

By contrast, the customers, the navy, were a conservative, restricting force. Working in the defense industry throughout my life, shoulder to shoulder with the military, participating in joint production of weapons and military equipment, I had a chance to compare the intellectual level of military personnel with that of civilian specialists. I arrived at this conclusion: the military are the most conservative part of our society; the most conservative members of the military are sailors. More than once I witnessed and took part in acute differences of opinion between designers and military men, but I never saw a deeper difference of approach towards military-technical problems as the one between designers and sailors, not between designers and land-based missile men, nor in aviation, nor in armored vehicles.

For example, at a conceptual meeting at the design bureau in Miass, the designers of missiles and submarines offered new, progressive concepts for developing the sea element of the strategic "triad." In response, the military suggested limiting ourselves to building some kind of a sea-based complex that was flawed, by many measures. Their suggestions could not be justified by a reduction in production expenses or by an increase in strategic efficacy. The military just equivocated, saying things like "We know better what we need." Factually, standing behind their words were simply poorly researched and biased orders handed down by the superiors. Kovalyov and Makeyev boiled over.

"Respected clients, what's going on!" Makeyev exclaimed. "It is your job to criticize us for poor, weak suggestions. We do our utmost, make profound explorations, offer you a missile complex with superb characteristics, we convincingly prove its expediency, and in response you, I am sorry to say, offer some runt!"

Makeyev nodded in sync with each word, as if he were hammering the words of his indignation into the desk, and outlined the size of the "runt" with his hands.

"I suggest that we trade suits with the military!" perpetually calm Kovalyov added.

He was unable to watch the elegant concept of a prospective complex fall apart.

"Who should be persuading whom to do better?" he went on. "Perhaps the respected military is operating with extremely high mental categories beyond reach for us civilians?"

In the "war of engines"—of military technologies—the authors of new technologies have better understanding of them than their consumers. Lengthy communication with the military at all levels—from marshal to soldier—just confirmed my opinion: military policy and military technologies should be created by civilians.

There came a period when Makeyev, having reached the highest levels in government, sensed that he had done everything he could in his field. The design bureau and missiles production worked like clockwork; the most sophisticated scientific-technical organization had been created; strong and worthy personnel had been pulled together. To cap it all off, a strategic supersubmarine, the Typhoon, had been built, with a new, solid-fuel D-19 missile. This was an underwater nuclear battleship—in fact, three submarines built into one hull.

At about the same time—it was bound to happen sooner or later—a warming up of international relations began. As a consequence, orders for new missile complexes declined. Makeyev's design bureau began to skid. In the end, the Typhoon, with its unique capabilities, turned out to be his bureau's climactic achievement. Many years of research by the best minds of the design bureau brought no greater result, and this was not their failing. The warm-up would inevitably change the military industry. The phantom of real disarmament loomed, but so far it was only a phantom. It was already quite clear that we were not going to start a war against the whole world, that military confrontation is not effective international policy. There were not absolutely clear signs of a change in direction, but there was something to talk about already.

It was in this period, when Makeyev and I were on a business trip to Altai Research Institute for Chemical Technology, that I had a heart-to-heart with him. There were numerous difficult challenges over building the solid-fuel engines for the D-19 missile of the Typhoon complex. After a long day of work, Makeyev asked me at dinner if I was in a hurry and offered to stay on and talk. We spoke about life, the future of the design bureau in Miass, families, children. Sensing the delicate, one-on-one nature of this conversation, the rest of our company quietly disappeared. We drank a bottle of vodka together. Makeyev got the second one. We drank it, too. I could see that two bottles was his method for untying my tongue, but this wasn't necessary. I would gladly have answered all his questions without the liquor.

After spelling out the overall situation in strategic forces, Makeyev showed that no clear future could be seen for the design bureau or for the military beyond this latest D-19 missile and the Typhoon. We agreed that in the coming years the design bureau might find itself in a difficult situation.

"And so, Vitaly Leonidovich, I am very interested to know what they think about me at the Central Committee in this connection," Makeyev said, cueing me.

I responded, "At the committee, so it seems to me, the leadership thinks that having conferred all possible regalia on you, they have paid all their past and future bills. There is nothing else left to pay you with: they will not give you a third Hero of Socialist Labor star. Your past is brilliant. Your elevator is at the top floor. The future is not clear, but I know for sure that the navy sailors and bosses at the ministry, at the Military-Industrial Commission of the Council of Ministers, and at the Central Committee are not going to replace you and won't help you get any other position. Your sea specialty is very narrow and specific. Being a leading manager, you should climb out on your own—you are prepared for it. But this is just my view from the side. Hell knows what the bosses really think."

"I more or less understand about the bosses. But what do normal guys think?"

"They think that when you get totally bored here, you will jump off from Miass into the Academy of Sciences. Or that you will become an alcoholic in your den without a family. These are not speculations but valid projections built on the basis of known facts."

"Are they mad? Where would I go without my bureau? I have value as the chief designer when the bureau is behind me. It's only after this that I am an academician."

Makeyev extended a finger to illustrate the relative importance of each role: first, designer; then second, academician. His voice even got coarse with indignation as he continued.

"Academician is a derivative from designer. The bureau is the main thing. I built everything there—it's my life. If we're not making missiles, I will take on city problems. We are not Miass proper, with its car factory; we are in an undeveloped area. Where shall we put the city? There is nothing except for the design bureau there. Everything is narrowly specialized. I will specialize in pickling cabbage if there is no other work for me. I'll make a big barrel."

"And what about this? It won't get in the way?" I asked, tapping on the bottle.

"How can you! Who slandered me in your eyes?" Makeyev demanded, as his eyes, big and bulging, almost popped with outrage.

"This opinion was formed, and apparently not without reason. I was instructed: check it out with him. . . . If there's nothing of the kind—thank God! But there is no smoke without fire. They even know who provides the drinks—your driver. You may endanger your driver very seriously: we'll have to punish him because of you. He is destroying the health of a designer on the most important strategic frontier. We'll hand the file over to the KGB, let them take measures."

"How can you, Vitaly Leonidovich! Even listening to you is terrifying."

I had a question on the tip of my tongue: Tell me, is it true or not? But he was going to lie, and it was not pleasant for me to push an academician into a corner and make him lie.

Instead, I said, "Viktor Petrovich, I understand your indignation. Nobody is going to tell you this except for me. I would have told you even without these two bottles. Somehow we never had a chance to be alone and talk. But now I am almost certain that you will stay in the bureau to the very end. I am a bit envious: I was not lucky; I was not able to stay on in the bureau to the end, in Dnepropetrovsk. My life was there, not in Moscow. And now my business assignment in Moscow has been extended, probably to the end of my life."

"But Vitaly Leonidovich, we are the lucky ones: to have a designer in Moscow at such an important position for us, instead of a party official. I will even tell you more, since no-one can hear us; if they could, they would say, these thinkers sing along thanks to a bottle! We all see you as a designer. And I think everything works very well between you and us. We are hearing advice from the top!" Makeyev said, pointing to the ceiling with his finger. "I have a toast, although we seem to have used up everything to toast with already, but still—

the last one—to a continued productive friendship! And off to sleep."
Unfortunately, my forecast turned out to be close to reality. Indeed, I
had to ask the local KGB to talk sense into the driver. And Makeyev's
wife called me more than once demanding that I take steps. She
called the minister, too.

It was proved long ago that the solitude of extraordinary people is
most often made more pleasant with wine. Makeyev was profoundly
lonely presiding in isolation on his Olympus. During long nights
in Miass, he tried to surround himself with people, but these were
mostly codrinkers and hangers-on wishing to get personal dividends
from their association with the chief designer. The chief's wayward
heart turned out to be his weakest link.

PART II

An Insider's View of Soviet Arms Development and Limitation

Almost all my life, I worked for the military-industrial complex. I not only observed the development of the Cold War processes but participated in them. I worked in design bureaus and was a specialist in aviation and missile systems, during which time I joined the Communist Party. After that, I worked as an instructor, head of a sector, and then deputy head of the Central Committee Defense Department. There, I supervised issues related to sea-based strategic weapons and was involved with various government defense agencies in crafting military policy and negotiating weapons reduction. As part of the interdepartmental working group, I directly participated in international talks, working out security concepts and preparing texts of treaties. All this gave me a special insider's view of arms development and limitation before and after the dissolution of the USSR.

CHAPTER 7

Military-Industrial Complex

The economy used to be divided into specialized subdivisions in the Soviet Union, including light industry, machine-tool construction, instrument-making industry, agriculture, and others. Branches that produced military products were grouped separately into the military-industrial complex. This group comprised nine ministries—Aviation, Machine-Building, General Machine-Building, Defense Industry, Radio Industry, Medium Machine-Building, Communications, Ship-Building, and Electronic Industry—as well as all research institutes, design bureaus, and plants which developed and made armaments and military technology.

The key feature of the military-industrial complex in the Soviet Union was the fact that the enterprises that made up the backbone of the defense industry belonged to the state. This was the situation until the Soviet Union disintegrated. The Soviet military industry was always completely closed. Specialists had no right to talk about their work. They had to sign a written statement to this effect. They are going to their deathbeds sworn to secrecy. Because of this, a most interesting period of history, unfortunately, is disappearing with this generation, without any prospect for recovery. I believe it deserves more interest from scientists and historians.

Absence of factual information about the military-industrial complex in the Soviet Union led to all kinds of myths and legends about huge military expenses, about the Soviet military-industrial monster, about a state within a state. A lot of such lies were made up to stir the public interest, but not for merely idle purposes. The image of a powerful military-industrial complex was created and maintained by joint efforts of the Soviet and foreign special services. These myths played into the hands of both sides.

Foreign analysts always inflated the Soviet military potential, envisaging a higher rate of allocations for their own use in a military confrontation. At the same time, the Soviet leadership presented the power of the military-industrial complex as a worthy counterbalance to threats coming from abroad. Besides—and this was the most important reason for flexing muscle—the Soviet Union's economic difficulties could be written off as a consequence of the "tremendous" military expenditure. The usual pattern was at work: when a leader is having difficulties, it is very convenient to unleash a small war using a plausible pretext. The Cold War and potential enemy strikes served as such a pretext.

Frankly, the shroud of secrecy surrounding the Soviet military-industrial complex played into the hands of American industry and similarly benefited other nations opposing Moscow. The secrecy did not do much for the Soviet Union itself, however. It had to try to live up to the high level of military and industrial power attributed to it, to live up to the level of a projected confrontation.

Many years of practical work of military-industrial institutes and design bureaus demonstrated that fresh ideas, new technologies, and new designs could emerge in the course of students' research or diploma design work. However, most of these ideas remained on paper. They got implemented only when their authors grew to become leaders capable of promoting the implementation of their early ideas (for example, ships on underwater wings or new designs of planes). Another reason that a decision on military production might be made was providing work for some concrete plant, for example. Keeping workers working was thought to be cheaper than restoring their lost technological skills after a break.

The absence of a comprehensive approach to implementing projects was a big drawback of organizing work at different military-industrial plants. The main attention was paid to the product that was being made and the newest technologies but not to the quality

of capital assets, though about 15 to 20 percent of the annual investment was spent on them.

For example, in the general machine-building industry, at one of
the plants, a lot of money was spent to build a very complex installation for testing in conditions of weightlessness. However, at the
same plant, barrels for tank guns were made on equipment used in
the 1940s and '50s. The straightness of the barrel was checked by
an old man. If he was ill, the guns were just not made. It was done
like this: the worker took a barrel and looked through it toward an
illuminated piece of paper on the wall. If he saw that the barrel was
not quite straight, he would bend it a little using a hand press. The
most interesting element of this technique was the sheet of paper
on which the local smart alecks drew erotic scenes.

The administrative-command system of the centralized leadership
of defense enterprises didn't stimulate them to grow. Growth of an
enterprise depended on whether the director and the chief designer
were ambitious people or not, and this depended on their personal
aspirations. But the director knew that his enterprise would always
remain a cell in a rigid military-industrial-complex structure. The
system did not make enterprises compete for quality. They knew the
state would never let them perish; that their plants would surely
get orders. The Central Committee and regional bodies would see
to that.

The directors of the defense enterprises were very powerful.
Among them were Supreme Soviet members, Heroes of Socialist
Labor, and highly skilled economists. But their high status was effective and suitable only for survival in the Soviet system in which the
employer, buyer, and investor were one and the same entity—the
state. After the Soviet disintegration, the plants that had no experience of work in market conditions were abandoned by the state.
The directors found themselves playing the role of circus bears who
were let out into the wild woods. Their skill of riding a bicycle was
of no use in the forest.

The picture of outdated equipment, status-based leadership,
and noncompetitive production was the same in consumer-oriented
industries. Annually, the military-industrial complex handed over to

other industries about one hundred thousand sets of documents on modern technologies. The Buran alone provided six hundred new technologies. But no feedback process was worked out, with rare exceptions. Strange as it might seem, the social factor influenced the quality of military hardware.

Scientific achievements in the Soviet Union, however, reached a high level. Money was allocated for this. We were not lacking in the newest military technologies. On the contrary, some of the newest effective technologies for killing people had to be stopped for human reasons, so that they wouldn't spread. Laboratories that achieved these high scientific results were carefully cleared away.

Scientific-technical progress was nurtured on the ideas of designers. This I know as a direct participant in the construction of small local systems and large, complicated strategic systems. Having successfully crossed the thresholds of basic research and development, new technology would often stall at the third stage—implementation and construction were not done on the same high level. Workers, technologists, and designers didn't provide high-quality work. There was a constant gap between a concept and its implementation in the form of a product. Bad quality began at the initial stage of production—the ore was of bad quality; metals and other materials were of bad quality. Then even the worst technologist couldn't be laid off from a plant. If this happened, it caused a lot of problems for the head of the plant. It was believed that laying people off made the criminal situation in the country worse. This couldn't be allowed. Let a delinquent work, even badly, but under a watchful eye. Everybody was obliged to work. The unemployed were caught and made to get jobs. This was the state policy; this was the policy of the party. For these reasons, many goods produced in the Soviet Union couldn't be competitive on the world market.

These weaknesses took their toll on military hardware as well. Deviation of materials characteristics from the standard made designers use more materials than they actually needed. For example, all flying machines in the Soviet Union were of poor quality in terms of weight compared with those in the West. The design and decorative coating were of low quality, and the specific load capacity was two times worse. This is why they were made twice as big. But this approach was impractical in radioelectronics. A chip couldn't become more reliable if made two times bigger in size. We had to install two or three chips. Here, the Soviet Union was lagging behind. For similar reasons, European military specialists considered tanks and self-propelled artillery made in the Soviet Union to be less effective than those made in the West.

In the military-industrial complex, there existed a system of leading design bureaus and prominent specialists in each key area: aviation, space systems, combat rockets, and ABM and air-defense systems, particularly strategic rockets. This group of enterprises emerged under Khrushchev, who thought that rockets could solve all military problems. There appeared temporary favorites among rocketmen due to competition between professional clans, personal relations, and the particular ambitions of leaders of state. Decisions on rockets were made without taking into account their military-political significance. Making decisions was not such an easy job for Soviet leaders because they had to reach some consensus.

For a long time, the Soviet Union did not have an official military doctrine. There were only a number of personal approaches. The army was not clearly defined; each defense minister regarded the army in his own way. Nobody tried to figure out how many weapons the army really needed. This led to poor understanding of the production capacity that would be sufficient for the military industry. The Ministry of Defense was always asking for as much military equipment as possible. *Gosplan,* the state planning agency, set deliveries on the basis of the country's economic possibilities; however, it gave priority to military orders. The military-industrial complex was obliged to annually increase its overall production by at least 2 to 3 percent, so production of specific weapons was not stopped even after the military's needs had been met. Also, a great number of design bureaus and plants made duplicates. The theoretical grounds for this was having capacity in the event of war, as well as creating competition, but, in fact, there was no competition in the Soviet command economy, where all enterprises were owned by the state and such free-market forces did not exist.

The use of weapons was not properly thought out either. The Central Committee Defense Department exercised strict control over production of weapons. However, once they were produced and handed over to the army, all control ended. Theoretically, the army was supposed to have its own body of control—its chief political department, which had the rights of a department of the Central Committee—but this was only theoretical. Control over the armaments was not a big concern of the army's chief political department.

All planning related to arms was a spontaneous process, but nobody was willing to admit this. In fact, this statement may arouse disagreement even now, but long-term planning, with the exception of individual cases, proved to be inadequate.

Even accounting for intermediate- and short-range rockets was not organized properly in the army. When we began to count these rockets for arms control treaties, we had to correct the figure we announced several times—we were unable to count, and account for, all of them, even though a nuclear rocket is hardly a needle in a haystack.

At last, in the mid-1980s, the Soviet military doctrine was worked out, and, in 1987, it was put into effect. The foundation of this doctrine was defense sufficiency. It attempted, for the first time in the history of our country, to outline the Armed Forces, along with deliveries of weapons and military equipment and, consequently, their production. That is, we were able to understand what military production capacity the country needed. This doctrine helped overcome some psychological barriers about the stockpiling of weapons and the continuous process of its production.

More attention began to be paid to the production of consumer goods at the military plants; production of consumer goods began to grow, approaching the level of military production. In the 1970s, military-industrial plants took up consumer-goods production only after they had met the military targets (at first, manufacturing facilities used raw materials that were waste products from different defense orders). Defense plants were given the following instructions at that time: yield of civil manufacturing has to be at least as high as the total wage fund of an enterprise. Seven out of nine defense-industry segments reached that level in two to three years. This period also saw changes in conscription terms and revisions of military-equipment supply plans on the domestic and foreign markets.

Science-intensive production was used not only for military purposes. In 1988, military-industrial complex enterprises accounted for 40 to 50 percent of consumer-goods production. In 1990, the figure was 58 percent, and, by 1991, it was 60 percent. These enterprises produced 100 percent of television sets, tape recorders, cameras, and sewing machines; 97 percent of refrigerators and deep freezers; 70 percent of vacuum cleaners and washing machines; 50 percent of motorcycles; and 22 percent of civil aviation planes, tractors, automobiles, tramcars, railroad carriages, ships, oil rigs, medical equipment, and diesels. It should be noted that fridges produced at the Krasnoyarsk plant, which also made sea-based strategic rockets, were sold in thirty countries around the world.

In order to improve the quality of the goods, experimental work was needed. In 1988, consumer-oriented research and development in the defense industry reached 25 to 28 percent. In 1988, 240 enterprises of machine-building for light and food industry were assigned to military-industrial complex ministries. This was done to improve the quality of processing equipment, which regularly had been losing 30 percent of the product.

The Soviet military-industrial complex's capital assets were worth 108 billion rubles in 1985 prices, which accounted for 5.9 percent of all the Soviet economy's capital assets. The government allocated 11 to 12 percent of capital investment to defense enterprises in the last years of the USSR, but this was not sufficient to maintain an advanced technical level. The value of the capital assets in defense at this point was not large because the defense industry part of the machine-tools and equipment sector was considerably worn out. Many plants used old equipment, even of World War II vintage. Capital investment was mainly channeled into new special equipment for laboratory work. The percentage of the country's total key material resources consumed by the military-industrial complex (VPK) for military-equipment production purposes was as follows: ferrous metal-roll, 6.0 percent; steel pipes, 1.7 percent; aluminum roll, 25.0 percent; timber, 5.5 percent.

What was the military-industrial complex's share in the USSR economy? In the mid-1980s, about 135 million people were engaged in the Soviet economy, which amounted to half of the country's population. All together, there were 5,100 design bureaus and technical institutes in the USSR and 3,200 scientific institutions, including 32 scientific complexes of the USSR Academy of Sciences. The military industry was concentrated at 1,770 defense-industry enterprises with a workforce of 10,450 people. This included 450 research-and-development and 250 design organizations. Eighty percent of these were situated on the territory of the present Russian Federation. Taking into consideration all these figures, we could say that the military-industrial complex approximately accounted for 8 to 9 percent of all the employment, scientific, and production potential of the Soviet Union. Readers may be disappointed by these figures, but this is the truth. I'd like to draw attention here to the fact that all the figures I use are not taken from newspapers; they are real figures I used in my work. Today, they are important historical data.

Not everything was well organized in the military-industrial complex. It was a conservative and fragile system which didn't allow for dramatic organizational movements. In some ways, it resembled an elephant in a china shop. Since about 80 percent of military production was concentrated in the area of the present Russian Federation, in other regions there were separate major scientific divisions, such as the Paton Institute of Electric Welding in Ukraine and the Glushkov Institute of Cybernetics (which developed electronic calculating machines), enterprises developing rocket technology, aviation, armored equipment, and radioelectronics. Latvia had the Institute of Organic Synthesis, which developed substances on the basis of bioorganic chemistry or gene engineering. Belarus had heavy automobile building. However, besides Russia, the biggest defense enterprises were developed only in Ukraine and Belarus—in those republics which were never expected to secede from the union.

Besides those people working within the military-industrial complex, another 546,000 were engaged in producing military goods in civilian branches of the Soviet economy. Still another 388,000 were engaged in maintaining and running military technology in the Ministry of Defense. All in all, about 8.4 percent of all the working people in the Soviet Union worked in the military-industrial complex. It accounted for over 20 percent of the country's gross domestic product.

Fifty-five percent of the overall defense workforce was engaged in the production of military equipment in the defense industry; the rest were busy in consumer-goods production or working in the social sphere. Out of all industrial workers engaged in military production, 33.7 percent worked in the aerospace complex; 20.3 percent worked in radio engineering, electronics, and communications; and 9.1 percent worked in shipbuilding. Also, 14.1 percent of the military-industrial workforce were engineers and scientists; 77.4 percent were factory workers; 7.1 percent were managers; and 1.4 percent were service workers.

In the 1960s, Brezhnev raised salaries in defense-industry scientific branches by 20 to 30 percent. Social problems at the enterprises were solved much more easily. It was important to take into account the fact that over fifty cities and towns of the USSR were almost entirely connected with the military-industrial complex. These increased salaries lasted fifteen to twenty years. In the 1980s, the salaries of defense-industry workers began to gradually lag behind those of workers in other industries. At this period in time, the international tensions began to ease. The army had received all the main armaments. This led to cuts in military orders and the beginning of stagnation in military production. There also existed a psychological factor for people working in the military-industrial complex, which not everyone was able to bear easily—the burden of secrecy. It was not easy to maintain a strict regime of technological discipline, meet rigid requirements for quality, and endure severe control. When money ceased to be an incentive and the social safety net was not as reliable as it had been, skilled workers began to trickle away.

CHAPTER 8

Communist Party

For a long time, for thirty years, which is almost half my life, I was a member of the Communist Party. Sixteen years out of these thirty, I worked at the Central Committee, in the party headquarters, dealing with military-technical problems in the Defense Department. After the disintegration of the Soviet Union, I was not a member of any party.

Membership in the party—as for the majority of Communists—was a formal and not very burdensome part of my activity. But it was excellent experience. Many processes in the country were initiated in the party cells at different levels. The most significant ones were initiated in Staraya Ploschad, at the Central Committee.[1] There were both positive and negative initiatives among them. Some of them developed before my very eyes.

As a person with a tendency to analyze things, I was very curious about what triggered the disintegration of the Soviet Union. It was an event of global significance, but for some reason, what kept coming to my head during the collapse was a trivial parallel case in one Transcaucasian republic. Newspapers reported that a big block of flats fell apart there. When officials took a sample of the mortar, it turned out that its main component was sand. Cement for the mortar had been stolen during the construction process. This subconscious comparison, I believe, is apt. The Communist Party was the mortar that kept the Soviet Union together. Once the cement of the party had been stolen, the Communist foundation was gone and the country disintegrated. The party turned into a bureaucratic organ—sand which didn't hold together anything.

The party's influence in my work experience cannot be easily described. I didn't see a big difference when I was working for more than two decades in the highest offices of the party as compared to my earlier work as a designer. The party's support can be compared to sugar in water: one couldn't see it but could constantly taste it.

One of the most important functions of the party was to fill key positions. The party found personnel for everything from high positions to rank-and-file jobs. The work of the party personnel department in the Soviet Union could be compared to the work of the gardener who grows flowers and fruit trees. Now, nobody cultivates them and the garden is full of weeds.

We can trace the methods of the Communist Party by taking my life as an example. From 1956 to 1960, I worked as a designer at the Omsk Aviation Plant, which built Tu-104 planes. Simultaneously, I did a lot of teaching. During those years I was chairman of the council of the plant's young specialists and worked in close contact with the plant's party committee and administration. But I was never offered an opportunity to join the party. I personally didn't pay much attention to it. Then I began to work on a project at a Dnepropetrovsk plant that made strategic rockets. I was doing a good job.

A month into my time in Dnepropetrovsk, my colleagues said to me, "Aren't you going to join the party? Be aware, no matter how well you work, you won't make a career if you are not a party member."

"And what am I supposed to do for that?" I inquired.

"Put together references and write an application."

"Who is going to give me a reference? Nobody knows me here."

"Write to your previous job. Ask your former colleagues to write a reference for you."

I did what they advised me to do. I received excellent references from Omsk. However, these were not formally recognized at the new place, although they were taken into account. In the party committee they told me, "You must find someone here to give you a reference." The process was already underway; I couldn't stop. First, I approached the man who had started this conversation with me, Ivan Dudnik. I asked him to write a reference. Ivan reluctantly agreed. But some time later, his wife came to me and said that she was against her husband giving a reference to a person whom he didn't know very well. If something happened to me at such an important plant, she felt, it would be her husband who would bear the responsibility. And they had a family, children. . . .

I went to talk with Ivan again and asked, "What's the problem? Who is going to write the reference? You or your wife?"

Ivan said that he would, but the wife was the problem. She was against his doing it. He thought for a long time in silence and then said that he would write me the reference. Things were easier with the second reference. A colleague who sat next to me immediately agreed to write it. From there on, the application process was all formalities and is of no interest.

Membership in the party was not burdensome. Practically all party meetings and committee gatherings discussed projects and designing which the plant's specialists were engaged in. They differed from regular factory meetings only in that the Communists could, to a certain extent, criticize the work of their bosses. And at regular factory meetings, the bosses criticized them.

The party committee—the *partkom*—was the highest party organ at the plant. At *partkom* meetings, one could engage in a dispute with the head of the plant and even go against his decisions. The *partkom* was supposed to give an approval when appointing or promoting any persons, not just Communists, to leading positions. It was also the *partkom*'s duty to distribute bonuses for work fulfilled. Membership in the *partkom* was an honorable position. It was recognition of the employee's high position at the plant.

The launch of the R-16 at the end of October 1960 that killed Marshal Mitrofan Nedelin and resulted in the biggest catastrophe in the history of Soviet rocket technology led to a personnel reshuffle at Yuzhnoye Design Bureau. A new group was set up for the R-16 rocket complex. It had taken almost eight months to carry out a technical analysis of the accident and eliminate possible causes. Mikhail Yangel, the chief designer, said after the investigation, "I need a ready-made specialist for this rocket, so that he can get into the work right away." By that time, I already had the reputation of a designer who was capable of not only coming up with a new idea but also drafting it, making it, and testing it, all very fast, which ran contrary to the conservative traditions of the Dnepropetrovsk bureau. But if I hadn't been a candidate for membership in the party by that time, I wouldn't have been eligible for acceptance into the group of leading designers.

The responsibilities of leading designer weren't clearly outlined. Each leading designer took on as many tasks in a project as he was able to cope with. For me, the role involved both designing and organizational activity. My head was brimming with ideas. But a leading designer did not have time to spend at a drafting board; that's why the ideas went to various designing departments for development.

It was quite a job to plant your ideas into the heads of those who worked in designing departments. These employees were also considered to be a technical elite. They kept a jealous eye on their rights and responsibilities. Sometimes serious disputes would arise. Employees from the designing departments would go to *partkom* to complain about me. The head of *partkom* would report to Yangel, the chief designer, who would solve the problem with me by discussing it and provoking me to voice my opinion about the proposals of the people from the designing department, as if we were designing together. Yangel was very open and candid. In the course of our conversations, he would describe the top leadership in Moscow, other chief designers, his deputies. These were highly interesting talks. Yangel had nothing to conceal. More than once when I was in Yangel's office, he received calls from Dmitry Ustinov after Ustinov became Central Committee secretary in 1965. Yangel would beckon to me as if to say, "Stay, you're not interfering in the conversation." Afterwards, he would comment on the part of the conversation that could be of interest to me.

The work on strategic systems went on under constant monitoring and control by the military-political leadership of the country. In addition to the Ministry of General Machine-Building, the Central

Committee's Defense Department kept an eye on implementation of the projects. Ustinov, who was head of the Military-Industrial Commission of the Council of Ministers from 1957 to 1963, and the general secretary himself, received information through the Defense Department. Simultaneously, the staff of the Military-Industrial Commission of the Council of Ministers also exercised tight control over work on strategic systems. The bulk of information came to this triad of governing bodies through the leading designer, who, in his turn, lobbied his interests in connection with the project.

A system of oral and written reports from the leading designer was worked out. We leading designers knew that we could give technical details to the Military-Industrial Commission of the Council of Ministers without fussing too much with editing. The reference memo or *spravka* for the Central Committee Defense Department, however, besides providing the technical outline, was always a sort of test for the leading designer (or any other person noticed by the Central Committee). This *spravka* tested the designer's ability to express his thoughts, single out the most important things, and pose questions that were worthy of the Central Committee's level. Together with the technical problem at hand, the Central Committee was studying the specialist who presented it. If the specialist got positive feedback on many points, his name was placed on a list of candidates for promotion, which each instructor at the Defense Department kept. The regional party bodies should have also practiced this approach taught by the instructors at the Defense Department.

The Defense Department got this name in 1954 after Khrushchev reorganized the Central Committee. In Stalin's time, the Central Committee defense-industry department was called "the personnel department of the defense industry." Its main responsibility was to find people for high-level positions in the Soviet military industry. The party exercised control over the work of the military industry through personnel. The Central Committee had its own retraining centers for leaders. This remained the department's main function later on. Special attention was paid to specialists slated to work in the administration of the Central Committee Defense Department. They were checked carefully from all sides. The turnover of personnel at the Central Committee was a very slow process. The people who had successfully mastered the specifics of work in the Defense Department stayed there for fifteen to twenty-five or even forty years, but not all of them.

The responsibilities of the Defense Department instructors included the following main functions:

- analysis of the incoming documents and information;
- research of new ideas and technologies in the interests of the country's defense and lobbying for them if necessary;
- oversight of the implementation of decisions of the Central Committee within the competence of the Defense Department, including decisions involving the defense-industry economy and the social sphere;
- examination and selection of personnel for key positions in the defense industry.

The Defense Department also had a say in awarding scientific degrees to leading and chief designers on the basis of the work they had done rather than on the basis of a thesis and its defense. In addition, it could recommend the level of state awards and bonuses for projects fulfilled. It could even have a say in solving some problems at enterprises, especially those concerning social issues. For example, the Defense Department might allow an enterprise to build a resort or sports facility, or allocate automobiles that couldn't be bought in shops. When I worked in the department, I, for one, helped the Dnepropetrovsk plant get a big cruiser yacht, the Konrad-45, built in Poland.

The Central Committee had always attached special importance, however, to the examination and selection of personnel. A list of key positions known as the *nomenklatura* was circulated in the Central Committee departments. Each industry sector of the department had a copy of this document. It listed three levels of positions: the most important ones were ministers, their first deputies, chief designers, and directors of the leading design bureaus and plants. They all were on the Politburo list and were approved by Politburo decisions. Ministers' deputies, heads of enterprises of a lower rank, and party committee secretaries of the most important enterprises were the purview of the Central Committee secretariat. Heads of the ministries' main departments and some directors of enterprises and heads of party committees were supervised by an appropriate Central Committee department. To some other positions, which were not on the list, heads were appointed after telephone interviews or talks with ministries' personnel-department heads or with the defense department of the appropriate oblast committee.

The *nomenklatura* list was a circulating document. The Defense Department always had a constantly renewed list of "reserve players"—candidates for replacing this or that leader. Specialists got onto the list of reserve players based on the results of a detailed discussion of their business and personal qualities. To some extent, this reduced favoritism in appointing people to key positions and added objectivity but didn't rule out mistakes completely. The most important thing was that there was no discrimination on the basis of ethnic origin, gender, or occupied position.

A position in the Defense Department was the result of very tough competition. In the 1970s, when I began working there, a candidate who was slated to work in that department was under consideration for two or three years. For example, candidates would have to demonstrate the self-discipline required at the Central Committee. At plants, employees would sign a pledge not to reveal any secret information, but not at the Central Committee. There, staff kept major personal archives, but no documents were ever lost. The KGB tapped offices and conference rooms. This was confirmed more than once by mistakes made by the KGB tapping specialists. They would begin calibrating the system when they thought there was nobody left in the offices. But specialists of the Defense Department worked longer hours than others at the Central Committee. All the specialists knew about tapping but only laughed. Sometimes they would put on a small performance hoping that this would be recorded and then reported to the leadership.

The Central Committee Defense Department also asked the KGB to check a potential candidate to assess his suitability for work in the Central Committee. The KGB did the job scrutinizing the work of the specialist directly at the design bureau through a network of its agents there. Later, I was able to name two or three design-bureau employees who were undercover agents involved in this process.

As was typical, the Central Committee took time to acquaint themselves with my personality, and when I joined the department I gradually mastered this technique of studying candidates. Here are some of its key elements. It was advisable to meet with the candidate unexpectedly to check whether he knew the state of things really well, whether he was still wearing a good suit and white shirt or whether he put them on only when visiting the Central Committee, whether he was a communicative type of person, and how much work he had to do. His strength of character was studied by taking him through elections to different party positions.

Only when I started working at the Central Committee did I understand why they wanted to make me a member of the party committee in the Dnepropetrovsk design bureau. It had been a directive from the Central Committee. I was slated to undergo the process of personnel selection that I would later come to utilize myself. I wasn't friendly with the party committee of the design bureau. For example, I said openly that I didn't think much of the state awards and that I would prefer monetary bonuses—too mercenary an attitude for a true Communist, in their eyes. I refused several times to become a member of the party committee because my workload was too great. I couldn't afford to waste long hours sitting at meetings of the party committee two or three times a week. My resistance became a scandal. Once, a member of the party committee told me that this would be the last offer to become member, that they would never offer again, but I refused again, before finally joining later. Also, at the staff of the Central Committee, they took on people whom they needed, even if the individuals objected. That's what happened with me. During the last test launch of the SS-17, in September 1974, I was in Dnepropetrovsk. I maintained contact with the testing range on a special phone channel for high-frequency communication. The SS-17 could be put in the Guinness book for its reliability. Not a single rocket out of twenty-six test launches crashed. The bosses were not very interested in it and consequently didn't rush. That's why designers were able to do all the work to enhance its reliability. I was interested to know if the last launch at maximum distance over the Pacific Ocean would bring any surprises. Although we had promised to prepare the rocket for launch on schedule, the rocket was delayed in leaving the plant. The captains of special ships which were to monitor the launch from the ocean threatened to leave the area because they were running out of fuel. All these problems between the plant and the testing range were settled by phone, and because launches were conducted at night I had very little sleep. In the end, this launch of SS-17, a silo-based four-warhead missile, was successful and this concluded its test phase.

At 9:00 am the following morning, there came a call from the Central Committee Defense Department. They congratulated the design bureau leadership on the end of the new rocket-complex tests and said that the leading designer of this complex, Katayev, was expected that day at 11:00 am at the Central Committee in Moscow. Chief Designer Vladimir Utkin was in Moscow at that time. The call was taken by his first deputy at Yuzhnoye Design Bureau in Dnepropetrovsk, Boris Gubanov.

"Get yourself quickly to the airport," Gubanov said to me. "Didn't have time to sleep? You'll sleep on the plane. They said they would explain on arrival. Most likely, they'll be offering you something. You've finished the tests. Now they are going to have you."

I got into the car they provided and then the plane. There were no passenger seats, so I was given the air hostess' seat, where I was unable to sleep. By the afternoon, I was in the Central Committee office. Yevgeny Krasnov, a department instructor and a wise man who came from a defense plant in Kovrov and who was referred to informally among colleagues as "Gavrilych," his patronymic, struck me dumb with his words.

"Look, we decided to take you to work in our department," he said. "We have known you for a long time. You suit us. You have some idea of our work. What do you think of the offer?"

"I don't like it," I responded. "I'm a designer and will always be. It's my work and my hobby—a happy combination. And here you've got a party body, and on top of the hierarchy at that. I said no when they offered me a chance to work in the party committee. And this is the Central Committee! No, I won't. This is not for me. There are plenty of people who would love to work here. Have them."

"You fool!" Gavrilych bellowed, jumping on his chair. "Who is talking about party work? Have we ever discussed party problems with you? Here, we deal with technology, too, but the problems are bigger and more interesting. And there are more ways available to solve them. You remember the railway complex that you and Yangel were trying to get permission for? You were a leading designer for that complex. You can do it now from here."

"You won't catch me leaving Dnepropetrovsk for Moscow! Dnepropetrovsk is such a wonderful city! I've got friends there, interesting work, my thesis is almost ready and has been checked in practical life. . . . Besides, my family will never agree. . . . I have a wonderful apartment. The apartment block is situated in the park, a Czech project designed for southern cities. . . . I've got a big garage. It took me two years to have it built. I've only just put everything in order. I'm always at work. My wife expended so much effort to do it all. . . ."

"Wife! What are you talking about? Who is the boss in your family?"

This kind of back and forth continued to no avail. The next person to work on me was Boris Stroganov, head of a sector. He used more or less the same arguments. I gave a flat no to these two. I tried to involve Yuzhnoye Design Bureau's general designer, academician Vladimir Utkin, but Utkin answered that he was powerless to do anything against the Central Committee. Stroganov went to a department head, Ivan Serbin. Serbin was known in the defense field under the nickname Ivan the Terrible. He had worked as head of the Defense Department since the beginning of the 1940s. The conversation with Serbin was tougher.

I tried to stand my ground again, but Ivan the Terrible brushed off all my arguments, saying, "Work! And what are we doing here, may

I ask? Being idle? The work here is more serious than yours. Thesis? The thesis doesn't matter here. The Central Committee takes specialists, not diplomas. This is no Academy of Sciences, you know."

Ivan the Terrible was holding my biography in his hands.

He leafed through it saying, "Your wife's maiden name written here is . . ."

"Bitus is her maiden name," I informed him.

"I can see it. Well?"

"She is Russian. Her father comes from the Baltics but has become Russian."

"Russian . . . How do you know?"

"I know! All the Bituses are Siberian collective farmers. My wife's father, Afanasy Bitus, was a railroad worker and was killed in the war. His brother, Ivan Bitus, works on a collective farm, keeps a cow."

"Keeps a cow? This means he's Russian?"

"Do you know any Jews who keep a cow?"

Ivan the Terrible shot me a glance above his spectacles.

"You have been dealing with rocket technology," he went on. "You've written here that you gave lectures on aviation. Is this correct?"

"Yes, organized by the Znaniye Society. I've been lecturing about modern aviation since I graduated from Kazan Aviation Institute. I've given the lecture over three hundred times. I'm an aviator and keep track of these things."

"Here, you're going to deal only with rocket technology."

"Look, I haven't yet. . . ."

"Also, you'll have to do what you're told."

"But I want to work as a designer and not as a party official."

"You will deal with rocket technology here."

I was trying to put in another argument, but Ivan the Terrible was pushing.

"What did you join the party for?" he demanded. "You must have sworn to fulfill all the party's decisions. Here you're invited to work in the party HQ and you're being biggety?"

This went on for about forty minutes. He would jump on his chair with indignation and lean across the table close to my face. And then I would have this silly thought, "Now he'll bite my nose off in fury." At the end of the conversation, he said something like this: if you don't take this job at the Central Committee, we'll put a brake on your career. There'll be no promotion.

This was a serious threat. The work of a leading designer could really be blocked in the Moscow "Bermuda triangle"—the Central Committee, the Council of Ministers, and the Ministry of Defense. One call from Ivan the Terrible would be enough. Besides, my total lack of interest in drinking bouts with officials from the ministries complicated my already difficult relations with some of them. There came complaints like, "Katayev takes a formal attitude towards his work." I could only imagine how glad all these people would be if my career became stalled! My arguments were exhausted. I felt a controversy was growing. Either I would be transferred, or there would be a quarrel.

"Well, what's there left for me?" I sighed. "I'll be honored to work in such a serious institution."

Serbin looked visibly relieved.

"Now you're talking! Apartment . . . thesis, . . ." he scoffed.

As a leading designer in the design bureau, I was used to independent work. Now that I was in the Central Committee, I found myself in an atmosphere with strict regulation of my activity. My salary went down by one and a half times. I lost a wonderful apartment and a circle of friends. My wife was crying with distress.

People who worked at the Central Committee were not allowed to establish economic ties with ministries or plants, or get dependent on them for anything. If this kind of relationship became known, people could be fired. Committee personnel had to stay unbiased to the utmost degree. The Central Committee staff tried to compensate for the restrictions imposed on their lives by allocating dachas and opportunities to buy books and foodstuffs that were in short supply, but this compensation didn't offset the losses. It only aroused rumors about privileges the party employees had.

In the Soviet Union, the Central Committee Defense Department was the expert authority which evaluated projects and decisions on military-technical issues. Controlling how these decisions were fulfilled was its duty also. A specialist with an active attitude was able to do a lot in his service if he worked at the Central Committee. However, old-timers kept a jealous watch over such upstarts.

Only high-level specialists worked in the Defense Department, and they worked at a higher level of operations even than at the defense ministry. The work at the Central Committee was similar to the work of a leading designer at the design bureau in that there were many problems to solve, but the framework in which they could be solved was narrower. Taking initiative, which was what a leading designer did at the design bureau, was discouraged at the Central Committee by old-timers. They demanded that traditions be observed. In my opinion, these were harmful for such a body as the Central Committee. That's why I categorically rejected their credo, "The work in the Central Committee means fulfilling orders." I tried to show personal initiative on many issues. Feedback was swift. Old-timers expressed their dissatisfaction. For some time, I was on the verge of slamming the door in their faces and leaving, but after a while, they put up with my ways. Only occasionally would they attack me, criticizing me for something I thought deserved praise. That's what happened once, on my fiftieth birthday, when I gathered colleagues at my place. There was one man from the region there— chief designer of solid-fuel motors, from Perm. He listened for some time to my colleagues speaking and then took the floor.

"What am I hearing here?" he cried out in indignation. "And this is said by the Central Committee officials! Cannot believe my ears. After what I have heard here, my respect for the Central Committee has dropped dramatically. And you, Vitaly, don't listen to them. Be active here the way you were before, when you worked at the design bureau. Your active attitude has always aroused respect with us, in the region. Hold your ground."

My colleagues didn't expect such sharp reaction to their criticism. They were displeased.

"Who's that? What did you invite a stranger for?" they demanded. "You're washing your dirty linen in public. We'll be able to sort things out among ourselves."

However, this unexpected friendly support from the Perm chief designer had its effect. My active attitude towards work began to bear fruit. I saw it. I got to know important information which made me take even more initiative. I was particularly struck by the amount of developed armaments which got stockpiled, grew obsolete, and were then disposed of. Plants worked nonstop. What did the military need such an excess of weapons for, when they couldn't be used under any circumstances anyway? I wondered.

It should be pointed out that subordination and conservatism made the promotion of military-technical ideas difficult. That's why military and civilian specialists were frequent visitors to the Central Committee Defense Department. They came for heart-to-heart chats. The specialists who worked at this department, though often lacking in scientific degrees, had knowledge, life experience, a liberal sense of tolerance, and practical skills, which enabled them to establish relations with both top leaders and ordinary people at the plants. They could talk as peers with academicians and workers. A lot of ideas were born during such conversations. This department was the final authority. There was no place higher. Of course, ideas were different and the department specialists did not always rush to help implement them. Sometimes, it took a lot of patience and tact to explain to people where they were erring.

The Central Committee gave orders to the ministries and the Military-Industrial Commission of the Council of Ministers. Usually, the orders were drawn up by a department such as the one where I worked. Such an order would customarily be signed by the head of a department, but a rank-and-file instructor of a department could also do it. Here is an example.

In mid-1975, Dmitry Ustinov, who was responsible for defense industry, held a conference on issues concerning further development of rocket technology. The issue to be considered was whether to keep liquid-fuel rockets as the mainstay of the Strategic Rocket Forces or to move to solid-fuel rockets. The industry was not prepared to swiftly reorient itself towards the production of large solid-fuel stages for rockets. At that time, solid fuel was used on antiaircraft rockets and on intermediate-range and short-range missiles, that is, on those devices that were easily transportable. The relatively short range of these devices made it possible to offset the poor efficiency of the fuel they used by increasing its amount. The missiles got bigger in size but remained quite transportable. However, this approach would not work for large strategic intercontinental missiles.

I prepared an analytical report for the conference which stated that improvements to silo-based launch sites would be of limited effectiveness in case of nuclear attack. Thus, I concluded in the report, solid-fueled, mobile intercontinental ballistic missiles would be the most reasonable option. Ustinov ended the meeting with the phrase, "Long live solid fuel!" From this moment, the work on solid-fuel missiles intensified.

Not everything was accomplished through formal means; sometimes I had to use informal methods. For example, there is the case of Ust-Katav, where an oblast committee took the necessary steps to address a problem after I simply talked to the regional first secretary rather than involving higher authorities. The engines of modern, piloted spacecraft were made in Ust-Katav at a plant where workshops had wooden mainstays built by a Belgian company in 1895. The ancient beams threatened to kill people who were assembling modern space equipment. When a spacecraft failed to dock on an international flight with a Bulgarian cosmonaut, due to a malfunction in space, I accused the first secretary of the Chelyabinsk oblast committee of insufficient attention to the problems of the plant, which had resulted in the diminished quality of the plant's production. After my accusation, a resolution was prepared together with the oblast committee on the development of the town of Ust-Katav. As a result, the town was rebuilt on a new site.

By the beginning of the 1990s, the defense-industry production facilities of the Soviet Union were significantly worn out. Twenty-eight percent of the production equipment had worked ten years; 21 percent had worked eleven to fifteen years; 16 percent had worked over fifteen years. This equipment didn't provide the necessary accuracy, reliability, quality, or social and ecological security.

During the first year after the Soviet collapse, budget allocations for buying weapons and military equipment were cut by seven and one-half times. Allocations for research and experimental work went down eleven times. This resulted in irreplaceable losses in the military-industrial base and in personnel. The loss of such well-organized intellectual potential, which was the military-industrial complex in the Soviet Union, was a loss for the whole world. It could be compared to the loss of, say, the Russian ballet or sports. It would have been more profitable for the world community if an irrevocable conversion had been carried out of the Soviet military-industrial base, if its rich potential had been kept and used for peaceful commercial purposes.

About the Soviet collapse: it was a major historical catastrophe. This dramatic political shift had extremely negative effects on international security, especially in European countries. Stable development was disrupted. The West had been scared of a Jumbo in a big zoo. Instead of patiently taming it, the West helped destroy the zoo and open the cages of all the animals, who were not only armed with teeth but infested with fleas: terrorists. Now the West is suffering the consequences of this mistake. The West had already failed to take advantage of an important buffer—Soviet influence on the Middle East. Instead, new unpredictable, uncontrolled nationalistic regimes are rising from the fragments of the Soviet Union. These are new threats to both Russia and Western countries. So far, there exists no acceptable concept of how to combat these threats.

In terms of dangerous consequences, the dismantling of the Soviet Union could be compared with the situation if NATO were dismantled. Just imagine it: the former NATO members going knocking on the doors of the Warsaw Pact countries. Would you like such a situation?

I'll reveal a secret: the common opinion of the military and civilian politicians of the Big Five—top leaders of the Soviet Union—was that the NATO of the 1980s, which bound member countries by certain military-political obligations, was a favorable factor in world security. I'm talking of the NATO that hadn't yet begun to swell dangerously and turn into a military-political cancer leading to the death of international détente, which had taken so much effort to achieve. Because of its earlier, positive influence, there were no objections to eastern Germany joining NATO. In one of their telephone conversations, Gorbachev asked George Bush, Sr., why he wanted to get unified Germany into NATO. "Well, just in case," answered Bush, and Gorbachev agreed with him.

I would like this discussion to be regarded as the opinions of an independent expert who had an opportunity to observe and analyze the results of upsetting a fragile military balance.

CHAPTER 9

Government Defense Agencies

The Central Committee and the Council of Ministers approved decisions for the state on military-technical issues. These bodies had a staff of highly qualified personnel to prepare such decisions. At the Central Committee, such specialists were concentrated at the Defense Department. The Central Committee Defense Department was built on a functional basis and was divided into sectors. Thus, there was a sector of general machine-building, medium machine-building, radioelectronics, etc. One of these was the sector of the defense-industry economy. For some time, it also dealt with issues concerning military-technical cooperation and arms exports. Five to seven instructors worked in each sector. In Gorbachev's time, a group of consultants was set up at the department on issues concerning arms limitation talks. As deputy head of the department, I supervised the work of this group.

The number of people working at the department ranged from fifty-six to seventy-six. Their ages usually ranged from forty-five to seventy. I was hired when I was forty-three. Old-timers grumbled, "Soon we'll have kids from kindergarten here." In the 1980s, the staff became younger overall. Looking back, I can say that this took a toll on the quality of the department's work. The balance between the radicalism of the younger generation and conservatism of the older generation was thrown off. Former heads of this department, Ivan Serbin and Igor Dmitriyev, had been able to maintain this balance. When, after ten years of work in the department, I made an attempt to leave, Dmitriyev was categorically against it, because the balance could be disrupted.

The best specialists of the Soviet Union worked in that department. Dmitriyev, when he headed the department, won a dispute with Yegor Ligachev over qualifications of specialists being hired into the department. Dmitriyev wanted specialists' professional qualities to determine their eligibility rather than their party work experience. Gorbachev supported Dmitriyev on this issue in his dispute with Politburo member Grigory Romanov. Once, Dmitriyev invited me into his office. When I entered, he sat smiling, nodding his head, softly swearing. I waited patiently.

"Do you know what happened?" he asked.

"What happened, where?" I responded.

"I have just been to Gorbachev's office. I told him that Romanov is against our hiring good specialists and wants party workers."

"And Gorbachev?"

"And Gorbachev said, 'He'll have to go f—ing out then!'"

"Maybe this is the right thing to do."

"But it would mean I fired a Politburo member!"

"He fired himself. As the defense industry head, he was no use."

Gorbachev forced the defense industry head, Romanov, who didn't live up to this position, into retirement.

Work at the Defense Department was the most intense of all the departments in the Central Committee. Through this department passed the major part of the most important documents, which were called "A special file." Every week the specialists of the department were updated on the new and classified scientific and technical achievements, so they were in the know about the latest things.

Sometimes, risking charges of insubordination, military men came secretly to the Central Committee with interesting projects. Some of their projects were accepted. Many inventors came to the Defense Department with their ideas. Most were legitimate but there were odd moments, also. Once, a healthy looking man got an appointment. He complained that the KGB was eavesdropping on his thoughts and he had to sleep with a pot on his head. We checked him. It turned out that he had persecution mania. A department instructor, a wise man, told him that he gave a command to the KGB to cancel the eavesdropping on his thoughts. Some time later, this man called and said that now he could lead a quiet life.

Arms specialists undertook many interesting projects relevant to consumers. For example, rocket builders, who did telemetric measurements, demonstrated equipment which made it possible to determine in five seconds whether a person was sick or healthy. Other equipment could determine within one to two minutes the sick organ from different spots on the ear. Still another set of equipment made it possible to treat specific organs using acupuncture. By the way, the institute of acupuncture was set up in Moscow as a result of the department's efforts. Medical research coincided with military technology at many points. This is why there was a specialist on medical issues working at the Defense Department.

The specialists of the department sometimes took upon themselves the task of working out complicated technical and organizational decisions. Using personal contacts, the department helped set up institutes and design bureaus to get allocations for implementing local projects. To speed up the implementation of projects, the department sometimes used party authorities in the regions, substituting for the Military-Industrial Commission of the Council of Ministers. For example, the Soviet Union reached a high level of designing nuclear warheads for strategic rockets; these were comparable to American warheads. The department got 100 percent credit for that. An expert evaluation prepared by the specialists of the Defense Department based on the results of their own research into a problem was sent to the Military-Industrial Commission of the Council of Ministers and ministries. They received target orders from the Central Committee. Submissions to the Central Committee were usually signed by the department head, although department instructors also had signatory authority.

State control of defense projects in the country was in the hands of two agencies: the Commission of the Council of Ministers for Military-Industrial Issues and the State Planning Committee (*Gosplan*). Senior officers of these agencies were in the rank of deputy chairman of the Council of Ministers.

The Council of Ministers' commission, more recently called the Military-Industrial Commission, determined the direction of scientific research, including fundamental research and experimental-design work for construction of arms and military equipment. About three hundred highly skilled specialists worked in the commission bodies. It was organized on a sectoral basis and was situated on the territory of the Kremlin. The decisions of the commission were binding for all ministries and departments.

Leonid Smirnov, Ustinov's protégé and former director of the Yuzhmash factory in Dnepropetrovsk, and then former minister, headed this commission for a long time. Ustinov had been Smirnov's patron since the two were students and was pulling him to the top (Smirnov told me this himself on many occasions). Yuri Maslyukov replaced Smirnov in this position. The last chairman of the commission was former minister of shipbuilding industry Igor Belousov.

Proposals on conducting scientific research and experimental-design work were sent to the commission by the Academy of Sciences, ministries and departments, scientists and specialists, and the military. The commission determined a list of the most important technologies. It was similar to the office of science and technology policy that exists at the White House in the United States.

The commission also gave recommendations on the hardware to be put on arms delivered to foreign countries under the agreements on military-technical cooperation. As a rule, the new hardware went to the Soviet forces first. This stinginess and excessive secrecy led to large losses in global competition for arms sales. In the late 1980s, our arms export policy was reconsidered. The list of hardware that could be exported was expanded.

The commission gave assignments to ministries, departments, and the Academy of Sciences on specific projects and scientific developments in the form of a document called the resolution of the CPSU (Communist Party of the Soviet Union) Central Committee and the USSR Council of Ministers. It was usually the Council of Ministers that issued the resolutions of the Central Committee. The

Council of Ministers had a separate department on defense work consisting of twenty-five specialists. Depending on the complexity, such a resolution could incorporate into one project about five to seven hundred enterprises. Each enterprise received a specific task and supplies. The ministries were responsible for providing financing. The document, which was marked "of special importance," looked like a tree, with the participating enterprises represented as big and small branches, and consisted of five hundred to eight hundred pages. The project was coordinated among all the participants. There could be as many as fifty to sixty signatures of heads of ministries and departments. Usually, it was not Moscow officials who did all the routine organizational work but specialists from the team of the leading designer heading the project from the design bureau, professionals who knew all the details of the project better than anybody else, who were easy to deal with and ambitious, and who had no psychological barriers and could talk with people at all levels.

It was good for Soviet enterprises to get into such projects because they could receive additional financing and could buy new equipment to support developments in technical and social spheres. On completing very important projects, enterprises were entitled to 2 percent of the cost of work to spend on bonuses for participants in the project. The quality of the work was usually evaluated by the military quality control. The secrecy of the work at enterprises was ensured by a special team of special service people which was called the "first department." In some cases, defense enterprises fulfilled work on the basis of simpler documents than the resolution, according to the decisions of the Military-Industrial Commission of the Council of Ministers, which had some financial resources for projects, too.

The results of major research and experimental work were usually looked into by an ad hoc state commission (headed usually by a Ministry of Defense official), which gave recommendations on its further use. State commissions were not free of the political and personal likes and dislikes that leaders of the state and the party bore towards heads of certain endeavors within military industry.

This favoritism, to a great extent, determined the progress of a project and the evaluation of the state commission. The work of the Military-Industrial Commission usually ended with the decision of the state commission and the launch of the arms for production.

Gosplan, the state planning ministry, dealt with issues related to serial production and deliveries of arms and military hardware. Planning was made on the basis of recommendations issued by the Military-Industrial Commission of the Council of Ministers, which examined the results of experimental and design work, and proposals of the Ministry of Defense and regional defense ministries. All the recommendations and proposals were put together in a single coordinated document in *Gosplan* headquarters (there was a special department in *Gosplan* for this purpose, the master plan department), which came out as a separate section in the general annual plan of economic development of the Soviet Union, which had the status of law.

Another ministry, *Gossnab*, was concerned with supplies. They dealt with furnishing all the parts for projects. The Economics Ministry had a department which dealt with control of export technologies and dual-purpose products. A special body, *Glavlit*, part of the state committee on publishing, was responsible for policing the mass media to avoid publication of secret information. There was also a special body, the State Technical Commission, which determined the level of secrecy of this or that hardware or equipment.

Before decisions were made on new technologies or projects, experts from the Ministry of Defense and the ministry institutes conducted a lot of evaluation work analyzing cost-effectiveness. However, nobody attached much significance to these analyses because the most important thing was to achieve good final results—at any cost. Despite the obvious cost advantage of heavy rockets, on the basis of other indicators, more expensive rockets began to be developed.

The Military-Industrial Commission of the Council of Ministers did not always provide complete impartiality when choosing priorities or protecting the process of decision making from personal influence. Also, the commission had only limited influence over the whole chain of development of a new defense technology. The commission mainly dealt with scientific research and experimental work, without looking into the more complex processes of bringing new defense technologies into being, fixing imbalances in production, and saturating the army with arms and military hardware. Neither did the commission have any say in arms planning. This function belonged completely to the military.

In the 1960s and 1970s, as well as the early 1980s, the decision to launch this or that major defense project was traditionally made by a small circle of the military-political leadership. In Brezhnev's time, besides him, three other people were part of this circle: Ustinov, Grechko, and Keldysh. In the 1960s, there existed a body called the Politburo Commission on Rocket Equipment. Brezhnev was chairman; Ustinov was deputy; Grechko, Vasily Ryabikov, Smirnov, and other ministers were members.

The professional backgrounds of those making decisions was of no importance and this led to serious mistakes. For example, in the mid-1960s, at defense minister Grechko's behest (and contrary to the opinion of the Science and Technology Committee of the rocket forces), work on railroad-based strategic rockets was suspended for ten years, which opened the way for the United States to build high-precision MX missiles. The state was obliged to overcome the consequences of this decision in a very expensive way: to enhance the security of all silo launchers of Soviet intercontinental ballistic missiles, to build mobile ground complexes of strategic rockets, and then to build rail-based missiles later. This was three times more expensive for the Soviet Union. Lobbying was also a big factor. Directors and general designers were able to favorably push the military hardware they were offering. In many cases, a decisive role was played by the political weight of the head of an enterprise and his ability to open the doors of top officials who made the final decision. Some designers were made members of the Central Committee. They were given scientific degrees without a thesis defense, just on the basis of work they did. With Ustinov's active support, the government allocated special quotas for them to be elected into the Academy of Sciences.

When Ustinov, the Central Committee's secretary and head of the defense industry, became defense minister in 1976, there was nobody to supervise the direction of the defense industry for a long time. All questions had to be decided with the general secretary, and it was not an easy job for the head of the Defense Department to get an appointment with him. Some important issues of the defense industry began to languish. The Central Committee needed to have a head of the defense industry, but it was not easy to find a replacement for Ustinov. The process dragged on.

Then the wise old-timers of the Defense Department decided to talk. As a matter of fact, the building in Staraya Ploschad where we worked was one of the relatively new buildings belonging to the Central Committee. The security services also had their premises in this building. The building was stuffed with bugs. All the offices were bugged, even our small conference room. Special amplifiers were installed to calibrate the system. It was difficult to conceal from skilled specialists the presence of bugging equipment. I don't think the bugs were planted to find out how staffers were criticizing their bosses or to bust a conspiracy. More likely, the top party leadership was interested in informal opinions of the wise old-timers. Our old-timers were very careful about what they said to the bosses. They spoke candidly only among themselves, being aware at the same time who they were speaking with. Often these talks were of no consequence, but sometimes they were organized on purpose, with the hope that they would be overheard. Usually, the same group of people got together in the office which I shared with instructor Krasnov. I made presentations during these talks, as this was my role. Old-timers openly voiced their opinions about the appointment of a Central Committee secretary on defense industry to replace Ustinov. To make things look natural, we used profanities when talking about bosses but gave good advice at the same time. This is how it went: "The general secretary doesn't understand anything in defense issues. He is still an agriculture man. He doesn't understand that the defense industry cannot remain without a leader. The head of the defense industry, due to the importance of this segment, must be a Politburo member. Because we have no head, stagnation has already started there. And it's only the general secretary who is to blame for it."

We were interested to find out whether our histrionics would work. We had results soon enough. Grigory Romanov, a Central Committee secretary and Politburo member, appeared in Staraya Ploschad. He was appointed to supervise the defense industry, but Romanov didn't become properly involved. Our performance for the bugs worked again. This time both the general secretary and Romanov were the targets of our attacks. Profanities were supported with good arguments. The general secretary must have received this information. Besides, the head of the Defense Department came and confirmed our assessment. That's when a decision was made to retire Romanov.

Another time, we got together on the spur of the moment and had a very heated discussion on Buran, the Soviet space shuttle. A. A. Burov, a very knowledgeable specialist who had a nose for new ideas, called this project "*buryan*" (weed), which had a negative connotation. Everybody began to attack Vyacheslav Krasavtsev, an official supervisor of the Buran project. Everybody saw its uselessness. Naturally, Krasavtsev saw it also. He hadn't been silent on this issue and had criticized the work on this project in conversations with the department heads but had done so only orally. This time the dispute was very heated. We shouted so loudly our voices got hoarse. We conveyed the following conclusion: the Ministry of General Machine-Building was not controlling the situation. Minister Afanasyev was carried away by what Glushko was telling him, but Glushko was not Korolyov. He was only a specialist on liquid-fuel rockets, a specialist in a narrow field. That's why he led the problem of space orbital transport into a deadlock. Everybody saw this deadlock, but nobody dared to stop the work. People thought approximately along these lines: Minister Afanasyev channels all the main resources allocated for space on Buran, which nobody needs. For this reason, another important space project will be deprived of financing and will come to nothing.

"Buran is the biggest subversive act in the history of our country!" someone concluded.

Here is where I joined in, saying, "Well, guys, this is a little too much! Making a saboteur of Afanasyev, I mean. He is one of the best ministers of the country! Is he a saboteur?"

"Yes! Yes! A saboteur!" they shouted all together.

A colleague who liked to cross every *t* added, "He is a criminal who didn't commit a crime, but a criminal who knew about the crime being committed and didn't take measures to prevent it."

I should point out that Afanasyev didn't stay minister long, after that discussion. Unfortunately, I'm the only one still alive from this performance, so now I can share the story of the famous Buran in detail.

The appearance of the American space shuttle in the early 1980s bothered our military and political leadership a lot. The Cold War was in full swing. All scientific and technical achievements in the United States and the Soviet Union were considered in terms of their military use. The evaluation of the shuttle's military and technical possibilities by our specialists demonstrated that this transportation vehicle was able to put one-hundred-ton cargos into orbit. It was a step on the way to developing an antiballistic missile (ABM) system in space. Americans were stirring things up, also. They kept the Soviet Union on tenterhooks at our talks on the ABM Treaty by threatening to pull out.

After one of the experiments Americans conducted with the shuttle, when it went down into the atmospheric layer to the altitude of sixty kilometers and then went up into orbit again, materials began to be circulated in the Defense Department on the shuttle's potential as a nuclear bomber. These materials cited data from our institutes' research to the effect that the shuttle, when in orbit, could dive above Moscow and drop an atomic bomb unexpectedly from the altitude of sixty to eighty kilometers. In such a case, the defense system put in place under the ABM Treaty around Moscow wouldn't have enough time to react. The Soviet military-political command would be wiped out, and Americans could easily take the country: a terrifying picture. There were many hypothetical variants of Soviet-American nuclear war. But for some reason, the most implausible threats aroused the greatest concern. Could the Americans expect that we would behave like fools? That we would stop at nothing, no matter what?

And we did not stop, as a matter of fact: we decided to build a system similar to the shuttle. The shuttle's design could be found in American mass media in every detail. Some details were misinformation, but some were the actual design, as if the Americans were saying, "Now, try and do something like this." And we did something like that with the Buran, but it was like the pot in that joke when a man who lived in the north saw an electric kettle, went into his igloo, tied a pot to the wall of the igloo with a rope, and waited for the water to boil. The Buran cost the country over $18 billion for scientific research and design and brought the country nothing but embarrassment.

On the American shuttle, the liquid-fuel engines, the hulls of solid-fuel acceleration engines, and the control system could be used again. On the Soviet Buran, all these systems were disposable. The American shuttle systems, including engines, could change over to stand-by systems. On the Buran, the liquid-fueled engines were overstrained, reducing reliability. The success of the only Buran flight was more luck than the reliability of its systems. This is why nobody dared to put it into space again.

But the most important factor in this decision was that nobody needed a second launch. Our ship had nothing to deliver into space. The Buran program was a bag of conceptual mistakes. All calculations—a multivolume program—were done with the aim of building systems of counteraction to the United States in outer space. This is why Buran's whole concept was based on the notion of necessity.

The multiple-use concept also failed. The Buran was designed for re-use of tanks and other elements. However, no diagnostic procedures were worked out to test the elements for readiness to fly again after an uncontrolled landing. Our tanks were expected to land on hard ground, not on water the way the Americans' tanks did. Nobody would dare to allow the use of tanks that had tumbled on the hard ground for another, manned flight. This was a huge step back compared to the American shuttle.

Here, it would be appropriate to ask, "And where were you, guys from Staraya Ploschad, looking? You are clever. You were the experts and your Defense Department was the highest authority making decisions!" This would be the right question to ask. On Staraya Ploschad, the power of bureaucracy got the better of the power of protest. The faults that would lead the Buran program to its death were lying right on the surface.

Knowing that any rank-and-file instructor at the department could write a report to the Central Committee, I decided to approach this problem from a different angle: not just attack the Buran project but propose a constructive alternative. Was I a designer or a bureaucrat after all? Why couldn't I show the bosses what could be done in place of Buran, what could be the next step to follow the American shuttle?

I discussed it with Krasavtsev, who said, "Nothing will come of it. But go for it. You're still young. We'll die and you will be asked why you let this happen."

I drew a picture of a space system, a spaceship, and went to Boris Stroganov, head of the general machine-building sector. Being a polite person, he didn't object right away but listened to what I had to say.

When he could stand my young drive no longer, he said, "You may be right. But they will come to us and ask, 'Where have you been all this time? Billions have been put into this program and you propose to close it now?' How are we going to answer, I wonder?"

"We'll say that time goes on and many problems have become more conspicuous," I replied. "That we could do everything better. And overtake Americans. Here is a picture of what could be offered to replace this project, if you trust me as a designer, of course."

"I cannot argue with you here. Write a note to the Central Committee."

I had already prepared the notes and produced them. Stroganov began to huff with displeasure.

"OK. You can leave it here," he sighed.

After a week, he called and said, "Please, come to my office."

I went to Stroganov's office and saw my notes to the Central Committee lying on his table.

"Well, Vitaly Leonidovich," he began. "Here is what you proposed, and here is what our head institute on rocket and space technology says. Do you see the signatures? Who am I supposed to believe, do you think?"

"From the bureaucratic point of view you should believe the institute," I answered. "But here we have an obvious case. We can use our brains. We have good enough knowledge."

"Knowledge has nothing to do with it. The leadership will only look at documents. Here they are. Do you see what's written here? The institute is not going to abandon its line, or else all people involved in this project must be fired. There has never been anything like this before. Do you see what you're cooking? Do you want this to happen?"

"What if we try to talk with the minister?"

"Go ahead. But he won't tell you anything new. I'm not talking with him."

Minister Afanasyev heard my arguments with a cunning smile on his lips. He had nothing against my technical argumentation.

"What would you like me to do?" he asked. "You want me to go to Ustinov and spill everything to him? Just recently I got a slap on the face from him for Chelomei and now you want me to go and do dirt on still another academician, Glushko? Telling Ustinov that Glushko has been leading us in the wrong direction. So, go yourself, smart guy, and prove it to him. You see my point?"

I was thinking about why in this country individuals did not matter, position mattered. But I also remembered something else, a souvenir, given to me on my fiftieth birthday by a friend with whom I used to work in Ukraine, head of the defense department of the Dnepropetrovsk oblast committee.

"Here is a present with meaning to you, Vitaly Leonidovich," my friend said. "Don't take offense."

He gave me a statuette of Don Quixote with an open book in his hands. This is what people thought of me. And it could be true. I was not trying to defend a thesis. I worked from morning till late at night. I thought nothing of bosses and awards. I went on vacations in winter to ski instead of going to a summer health resort. In summer, I would go to the north sailing, sleeping in a tent. This was not very respectful of the design-bureau patricians. I was trying to change the scheme of rocket design. I was a geek. All the chief's deputies were against change; I was the only one in favor—a regular Don Quixote. But Don Quixote was not a bad person. He was proud and passionate. Was I aggressive and passionate? Undoubtedly. I managed to push some ideas through. Was I proud? My wife would scold me for total lack of ambition.

If I was a Don Quixote, I had to live up to that image. So, little by little, I was getting deeper into the concept of the new multiple-use space system. All the best that had been achieved in aviation and rocket technology was concentrated in it. I was sure that if the g-force secret wasn't discovered yet for some time, the concept of the space lift would triumph—an air-space system which I was proposing. But this is a special conversation.

Issues of special importance were heard at the meetings of the Defense Council. Both military and civilian specialists could have their say there: chief designer, director of the head institute of the industry, director of the institute of the Ministry of Defense, ministers, and representatives from *Gosplan* and the Military-Industrial Commission of the Council of Ministers. The general secretary of the Central Committee, who was responsible for the defense industry, always spoke there. His speech was prepared by the Central Committee Defense Department. However, the meetings of the Defense Council were not held very often. The time was always postponed. The meetings didn't facilitate the process. It was clear that this body played only a formal role in the procedure of making decisions.

Here is how the decision was made on two important defense projects: the SS-17, my last rocket at the Yangel design bureau, and its alternative, the SS-19, made by the Chelomei design bureau.

Design projects for these Multiple Independently Targetable Reentry Vehicles or MIRVs were given to both design bureaus for competitive development by the Military-Industrial Commission of the Council of Ministers. Yangel proposed a rocket which carried four warheads, was placed in a special container at the plant, and was launched from this container. Chelomei proposed a rocket with six warheads and a conventional launch system. The results of their work were investigated at a meeting of the Military-Industrial Commission of the Council of Ministers. Opinions differed. People were at a loss as to which project to develop. The arguments were mostly conceptual. The first disputable issue was the number of warheads. Was it better to have more or fewer warheads on one rocket? The Yangel design bureau had a design of a heavy rocket of the SS-18 type which could carry as many as forty warheads, but it was not even proposed. The design-bureau specialists understood that sooner or later the limitation of strategic arms would concern the number of warheads, so placing a large number of warheads on one rocket was not the best decision. Another issue was the launch system. Yangel's rocket, which was kept in a solid launch container, would be better protected from a nuclear strike and could remain in operation for a retaliatory strike. Chelomei thought that his rocket was meant to be launched on warning, so it wouldn't need enhanced protection and could be launched conventionally.

Smirnov, chairman of the Military-Industrial Commission, who knew all the arms problems very well, tried to explain to Defense Minister Grechko why we needed to enhance the survivability of our rockets. Smirnov, like many specialists, believed that nobody would push the nuclear launch button only on the basis of signals coming from the early warning systems. Malfunctions of these systems were not rare. This is why all strategic rockets had to be prepared for a retaliatory strike. On Smirnov's request, a mock-up of the silo launching pad, which had a high degree of protection, was made. Smirnov told me that he invited the defense minister and tried to demonstrate to him why it was necessary to enhance protection of a launching pad with a rocket.

Grechko was only half listening at the time and then said, "Give this mock-up to me. I'll give it to my grandson to play with."

It should be noted that specialists, including supporters of launching on warning, understood that a nuclear strike on Soviet territory could destroy the major part of our retaliatory force, our command and control points, and the country's leadership, together with the red button. This is why a stand-by system of combat control was set up which consisted of special command rockets. If nuclear explosions occurred on the territory of the Soviet Union, these rockets could analyze the situation and then be launched into the zenith, and from there they could duplicate the launch command for the other Soviet rockets.

Another Soviet superproject, which was also intended to address the problem of combat control after total destruction, was called the Dead Hand. It was a self-regulating automatic system which gave a command for the launch of retributive nuclear rockets in the event that all strategic command was eliminated. This system was to register and record information about a nuclear attack from the early warning systems, do an independent analysis of the nuclear situation after the nuclear explosions had occurred, compare all the factors and time, wait, and then give a command for launch of retaliatory rockets and indicate the targets. But introduction of this system meant that the fate of humanity would be passed to computers, so it was abandoned.

There were numerous cases in the Soviet Union when, after considering new military projects, a decision was made to reject very effective combat technologies whose use was recognized as inhumane or excessively dangerous if they went out of control. The laboratories where they had been developed were completely destroyed in these cases and the specialists were transferred to other projects. There were similar calls to reject nuclear weapons at the moment of their creation, but these were not heeded. The dangerous arms spread worldwide, and we don't know the end of this story yet. They won't be used for military purposes, but nuclear terrorism is a real threat. God help us to avert it.

But let's get back to Yangel and Chelomei and their rockets. The chairman of the Military-Industrial Commission of the Council of Ministers, Smirnov, understood that the argument about these two rockets was broader than simply which one of them to choose. Grechko and Afanasyev (contrary to the opinions of his expert institute and his first deputy, Georgy Tyulin) were in favor of Chelomei's project. Ustinov, Smirnov, and Keldysh were in favor of Yangel's rocket.

Ustinov and Smirnov arranged with Leonid Brezhnev to raise the issue at the Defense Council. The Defense Council's meeting looked into this issue in July 1969. The meeting was held in the Crimea, in the mountains above Yalta, in a hunting lodge. About fifty people were invited, including Central Committee officials, ministers, and some chief designers. They gathered on the seashore and then started off in a big convoy of government automobiles heading into the mountains. The front car was zig-zagging at a high speed on the mountain road. The others were trying not to lag behind. Passengers were being tossed from side to side.

They began to grumble, "This macho man will kill himself and us into the bargain. Let's drive slower."

Their driver was snickering, but when the grumbling grew louder he suddenly admitted, "Leonid Ilyich himself is driving! That's his usual style."

Anyway, they reached the destination safely. Brezhnev, excited, got out of the car.

"Well, how did you like my driving?" he asked.

Happy that everything had ended well, the people spread their hands and said, "First class!"

The staff of the hunting lodge was replaced by KGB people. The tables were laid outside. Brezhnev conducted the meeting. Lieutenant-general Mikhail Kozlov kept the minutes. Serbin, head of the Defense Department, was assisting him.

Yangel was the first to speak. He put forward a special strategic concept for his project. Yangel said that launch on warning is an unrealistic idea, that only launch on attack, after the explosions of enemy nuclear warheads on our territory, is possible. For an adequate launch on attack, we needed to reconstruct our launching pads in a way that would protect them. He thought that we needed to disperse rockets with smaller numbers of warheads in case the Americans began to negotiate limits on the number of warheads that each side is entitled to possess. Yangel cited concrete examples of ways to use "know-how" to enhance rockets' survivability, including "mortar launch." He gave figures cautiously, leaving some margin for himself.

Chelomei was the second to speak. His rocket was better, according to him, because it had six warheads, compared to the four Yangel proposed. He made it clear that he didn't think it necessary or expedient to enhance the rocket's survivability on the ground. He thought we were perfectly fit for a launch on warning. His speech sounded more like an advertisement. He was giving too high an evaluation of the rocket.

Minister Afanasyev was lobbying for Chelomei's project.

He didn't refrain from speaking out against Ustinov, saying, "Unfortunately, Ustinov joined the group of the opponents of Chelomei's rocket. This interferes with our work very much."

Ustinov wouldn't forget that attack.

The director of the leading rocket institute of the industry, Yuri Mozzhorin, gave a detailed independent analysis of the two projects. His conclusion was that Yangel's project was preferable.

Then the president of the Academy of Sciences, Keldysh, took the floor. He pointed out that the stumbling block was not the rocket but the doctrine. It was not quite clear what our ideology was. Would we be the first to strike? Would we launch on warning or on attack?

"Some politicians," he said in his usual quiet manner, "still hope to destroy the enemy with one blow. This is not feasible. We must ensure the technical possibility of carrying out launch on warning. It is the only way of keeping the United States from the temptation of using nuclear rockets."

Other speeches, from military specialists, simplified the whole approach: the rocket that carries more warheads is better.

Brezhnev listened without making his attitude clear. There was no consensus. On the contrary, the discussion was drifting into more and more complicated conceptual spheres. The general secretary wasn't prepared for that. Brezhnev announced a break. He beckoned Ustinov and Grechko to come over and began to reproach them:

"You should have discussed all this beforehand. Now look what situation you put me in," he complained.

The two responded that they couldn't come to an agreement.

An army general, head of the military's political department, Aleksei Yepishev, came up to them and said, "Leonid Ilyich! Why should industry dictate to us, the military, what arms we need? We know better what we need, don't we?"

They just brushed him off. The break came to an end. With a displeased look on his face, Brezhnev said that the draft of the decision of the Defense Council aroused objections and needed to be rewritten.

"I propose to entrust this to Ustinov, Keldysh, Serbin, Nikolai Alekseyev, and Mikhail Kozlov," he announced.

Brezhnev's dissatisfaction also manifested itself in the fact that, contrary to tradition, no dinner with toasts and lavish food followed. Designers, the military, and officials quietly left. Keldysh took the initiative in finalizing the decision of the Defense Council. He suggested formulating first, in the most general terms, the state's military doctrine. Knowing that it would be impossible to overcome the ambitions of ministers and that Brezhnev wouldn't want to aggravate relations with his entourage, he suggested passing a decision which would satisfy both sides: approval of both projects, though it would be hard on the country.

Ustinov and Keldysh wrote the decision. Serbin, Alekseyev, and Kozlov were assisting. They were writing it, on the veranda, the whole afternoon and then the greater part of the night as well. Since then, by the way, Ustinov and Keldysh have maintained friendly relations. By morning, the document had been typed and given to Serbin, who was to get the signatures under the document. It was decided that Grechko would be the first signatory. Serbin went down to Grechko's dacha. On seeing Serbin, Grechko disappeared into the park through a side door. He was nowhere to be seen for several hours. Serbin waited patiently. Eventually he managed to convince the marshal of the proposed solution. After Grechko signed, it was much easier to get all the other signatures.

The resolution of the Central Committee and the Council of Ministers of August 19, 1970, on launching these two rockets had a detailed preamble which said that the Soviet Union adopted the

doctrine of a launch-on-warning nuclear strike. This is how important decisions were made in the Soviet Union—by a small circle of
people. In Brezhnev's last years, such decisions were made by Yuri
Andropov, Andrei Gromyko, and Ustinov, after which Konstantin
Chernenko would get Brezhnev to sign the documents. Only in the
second half of the 1980s, during Gorbachev's time, did the procedure
of making such decisions begin to become unbiased.

CHAPTER 10

Interdepartmental Working Group

The Soviet military-political leadership significantly changed their views on the issues of practical arms limitation and cuts in the mid-1980s. There were a number of reasons for this change, but one of the most important was that Mikhail Gorbachev came to power. He had a new attitude towards foreign policy and the role of arms. Other factors in the military-political situation and security of the Soviet Union also changed.

Unlike Brezhnev, who visited all the country's biggest military plants, looked into the technical characteristics of weapons (I saw this with my own eyes when I accompanied him around workshops in Dnepropetrovsk as a designer), and knew all the main types of weapons, Gorbachev knew about military hardware, as well as the problems of foreign policy, mainly from reports. He didn't consider himself to be the best-informed person on these issues. This is why, for the first time in the history of the Soviet Union, the highest-skilled professionals were summoned to prepare decisions on complicated military-political issues. These were specialists capable of doing comprehensive analysis, of organizing and brainstorming. A narrow military approach towards the most important matters gave way to a broad, unbiased approach. This step should be registered in the positive column of Gorbachev's record.

At the same time, there was the growing threat of American deployment of intermediate-range and short-range nuclear rockets. During the Cold War, the Soviet Union's leaders failed to understand that their moves were bound to trigger reciprocal moves on the other side, which didn't improve the security of the country. On the contrary, they dragged the Soviet Union into a dangerous strategic stalemate. This was the result of the practice of leaving a narrow circle of military-political leaders to make major strategic decisions, without allowing system-analysis specialists to work out solutions. When Gorbachev came along, there developed an atmosphere of more freedom. Specialists were able, at last, to give opinions contrary to the old common notion that the leadership knows better. (Minister Afanasyev used to say, for example, "My institutes must be able to support my opinions.")

Once, at a Politburo meeting, Brezhnev shouted from his seat to Commander-in-Chief of the Strategic Rocket Forces Nikolai Krylov, who came out to make a report, "Nikolai Ivanovich, what are you going to say? You still don't know what I think on the issue you're going to dwell on." And that's how it would go. Specialists were not allowed to mix with people of power who made decisions. This brought about missed opportunities when the development of the military-political situation could have been changed had there been a different system of making decisions. A different decision-making system could have given opportunities to solve some domestic problems, too.

It was Gorbachev's democratization that enabled specialists to voice their opinions in the most important area—foreign military policy. Lev Zaikov replaced Romanov as head of the defense industry. He helped set up an effective five-level structure of preparing and approving decisions on all military-political issues. This system's five levels, from lowest to highest, were as follows:

1. Institutes and design bureaus
2. Ministries and departments
3. Interdepartmental working group
4. Politburo Military-Industrial Commission (which included heads of the Ministry of Defense, of the General Staff of the Armed Forces, of the Ministry of Foreign Affairs, of the Military-Industrial Commission of the Council of Minis-

ters, and of the KGB, as well as the secretary of the Central
Committee for industry and the military-industrial complex)
5. General secretary of the Central Committee

The interdepartmental working group was founded and officially
endorsed in 1986. I myself worked out the document. It was signed
by Zaikov, Viktor Chebrikov, Eduard Shevardnadze, Sergei Sokolov,
Anatoly Dobrynin, and Yuri Maslyukov. Gorbachev signed the document in May 1987. The document specified who would be members
of the interdepartmental working group and what departments they
represented. Sergei Akhromeyev and Nikolai Chervov represented
the Ministry of Defense and the General Staff of the Armed Forces;
Yuli Vorontsov and Viktor Karpov represented the Ministry of Foreign
Affairs; Vladimir Kryuchkov represented the KGB; Nikolai Detinov
represented the Military-Industrial Commission of the Council of
Ministers; Georgy Korniyenko and Viktor Starodubov represented
the International Department of the Central Committee; and I myself
represented the Defense Department of the Central Committee. The
working group usually gathered together thirty to fifty people.

The interdepartmental working group had a right to make independent decisions on military-technical issues. All opinions of dip-
lomats, industries, and the military were discussed at its sessions.
When these decisions were registered as protocols, they were sent
to departments to be implemented. The interdepartmental working
group formulated opinions which were then sent to the Politburo
Military-Industrial Commission and to Zaikov. After that, the materials that had been discussed were approved in the form of Politburo
resolutions.

Usually, five people would sign the draft Politburo resolution,
but sometimes as many as eight, including Zaikov, Shevardnadze,
Chebrikov, Kryuchkov, Maslyukov, Igor Belousov, and Oleg Baklanov.
Gorbachev signed it without gathering a Politburo meeting, because
already there were serious signatures on the document. Signing was
a kind of de facto voting. Not a single mistake was made over the
whole period of the work of Zaikov's commission and the working
group. There were mistakes, of course, in the foreign policy, but

only when the issues didn't concern the working group. Out of thirty to fifty people who came to its meetings, anyone could speak out. This was very effective. The interdepartmental working group didn't have a head who could impose his opinions on others. We had a coordinator only. Any member could invite the others to gather at his office, and in that case he was the coordinator. This made it possible to come to an impartial solution of a problem.

The interdepartmental working group had to look into quite a number of different problems. These could be simple things. For example, in Votkinsk, the Americans who inspected intermediate-range missiles had their phones disconnected. This problem was settled by the working group within two or three minutes. There were other questions, however. The American side asked for permission for its specialists to visit the northern testing range, where, allegedly, underwater caves were being built to hide submarines. The Soviet side had been trying to assure Americans for a long time that there were no hiding places in the northern testing ground, but the Americans were insisting on an inspection trip. Then the working group made a decision to let them visit the site. There was nothing to see there. The American team came to the north certain that shelters for submarines had been built. They even brought equipment for underwater work. The situation looked comical when they entered a cave and saw that there was no water in it.

The working group also discussed the issue of "open skies," which later became more widely familiar when the Treaty on Open Skies was signed in 1992. We never, ever lied to the Americans—neither during talks, nor during inspections, nor during joint tests. The working group always looked into all the Americans' possible objections. When Americans proposed something during talks, the group never offered any argument. They just said, "That's what the American side thinks." We always tried to take into account all possible opinions and the opponents' possible reaction. This method gave the best result. For example, the first Strategic Arms Reduction Treaty (START I), with the 50 percent cuts, wouldn't have been accomplished if we hadn't gone deep into the technical details. The treaty consists of 804 pages, 800 pages of which contain technical data. The fact that this treaty was accomplished is to the credit of technical specialists, not politicians, because technical specialists who represented the military-industrial complex solved all technical issues related to the treaty.

From my position in the interdepartmental working group, I was able to observe some interesting characters and interactions involved with arms limitation.

The Ministry of Defense and the Ministry of Foreign Affairs had always been the main opponents over weapons cuts. They alone would never have come to an agreement, because this was a confrontation regarding the issue of war and peace. The Ministry of Defense thought that peace could only be won by force. The Ministry of Foreign Affairs believed that the time for force had passed. In fact, the attitude of the Ministry of Foreign Affairs was more progressive.

The KGB in our group was represented by Nikolai Leonov. He spoke only when he was made to. More often than not, the KGB was mute. The representative from the Military-Industrial Commission of the Council of Ministers spoke up only when his opinion was needed about the technical side. So, the main decision-making trio was composed of the representatives from the Ministry of Foreign Affairs, the Ministry of Defense, and the Central Committee Defense Department.

Sergei Akhromeyev was the senior person from the Ministry of Defense and the General Staff of the Armed Forces. He lobbied for all the stands taken by the military. His emotional attitude led to grave mistakes. He once told Americans that our heavy bombers could carry twelve cruise missiles, though they could carry sixteen. Akhromeyev had known the number before. I remember sitting in his office when he made several telephone calls to find out how many cruise missiles our heavy bombers could carry. When the aviators answered him, he even switched on the speaker so that we could also hear. He knew that the bombers could carry sixteen cruise missiles exactly, but here he was telling Americans this other figure—twelve. Americans had already known the true figure, but wrote down his answer as an official number. We had to disavow his statement within a year.

I said to him, "Sergei Fyodorovich, how could you have made such a mistake?"

And he answered, "And what do you want, Vitaly Leonidovich? I have to sleep on a hard bench in the anteroom, my head leaning on the wall, while bosses sit talking there. What can my head produce?"

Akhromeyev admitted his mistake. Unfortunately, such mistakes happened.

All the main questions of military policy of the late 1980s (except the unification of Germany and the pull-out of troops), including international military détente, passed through the interdepartmental working group. The structure worked smoothly, covering a wide range of issues, including military-technical problems, openness, border talks, etc. (except withdrawal of troops). Attracting specialists from military and civilian institutions and design bureaus and heads of all interested security agencies at all stages of practical work prevented frictions. The specialists understood the independent logic of events. They spoke a common language and saw each other as equals. Specialists were not just dummy opponents but direct participants in working out concrete steps towards arms limitation on a state level, even though this process in a number of cases would undermine the very existence of many design bureaus and industrial organizations.

One can judge the effectiveness of the interdepartmental working group by the number of "products" it released. Within a year, it analyzed 2,500 cipher telegrams and operational diplomatic documents and prepared and passed eighty to ninety resolutions of the Central Committee Politburo on concrete military-political issues. It conducted all practical hands-on activity in eight areas of the Soviet Union's negotiations on military-political problems.

Even now, one comes across nostalgic notes in the Russian mass media about the smooth work of the interdepartmental working group in Gorbachev's time. My job on international talks (START, etc.), before Zaikov came, was to write long reports about the state of the talks. One column was headed, "The attitude of the Soviet side"; another, "The attitude of the American side"; the next, "What's to be done in this situation." These reports went to the leadership, who didn't read them, of course.

But when Zaikov came, he immediately saw this very serious aspect of the activity of the Defense Department and said, "Please, get ready and we'll meet to discuss this particular issue."

Several days later, Zaikov invited me to his office. When I came in, I saw Maslyukov there. At that time, Maslyukov was deputy chairman of the Council of Ministers, and chairman of the Military-Industrial Commission of the Council of Ministers. Zaikov asked me what I could suggest. I replied that the redundancy of armaments was a bad thing, but it was only one part of the problem. Our biggest miscalculation was when our own rockets—intermediate- and short-range missiles in Europe—became a threat to the Soviet Union itself.

Formally, it was Americans who proposed to fully eliminate intermediate-range missiles: the zero option. Ronald Reagan, the master of complex moves, stood to gain no matter what. If the missiles were eliminated, he would get credit for being the author of a major foreign policy move toward peace. If the Soviet Union rejected his proposal, he could simply say this confirmed his statement that the USSR was an evil empire. The majority of our specialists believed that Reagan was banking on the second possible outcome, that Moscow would reject the U.S. proposal.

Gradually, the military and civilian specialists in Moscow began to understand the necessity for the Soviet Union to finally get rid of both American and Soviet nuclear intermediate-range missiles. They began to understand that intermediate- and short-range missiles were much more dangerous for the Soviet Union than for the United States. With the American Pershing II missiles aimed at Moscow and capable of flying there from Germany in eight to twelve minutes, the Soviet leadership wouldn't have enough time for making a retaliatory decision. The military saw this very well, but didn't even think of taking any practical steps in the direction of cutting these missiles. Heated discussions began in the General Staff of the Armed Forces and in the Central Committee, long conversations with Valentin Varennikov, then the first deputy of the chief of staff, and with Akhromeyev, chief of staff. They rejected categorically the arguments and logic for cutting armaments at that time. The complete turnaround from stockpiling weapons to cutting weapons was a totally unexpected and strange notion to them. I had the impression that Varennikov was the first to take a pragmatic view of the issue, but he was immediately sent to Kabul as a representative of the General Staff of the Armed Forces. Akhromeyev took the first real steps towards elimination of intermediate-range missiles as a personal tragedy.

The Soviet defense minister, Marshal Sokolov, supported Akhromeyev in opposing Gorbachev's drive to cut arms. The two would corner me in a quiet office in the Central Committee building before a meeting and ask about the new policy.

"Can you tell us where these outrageous goings-on come from? Trying to eliminate almost new nuclear missiles which the USSR had so much trouble building! It's a crime against the state!" they would say. "We have no intention of participating in it. We remember Khrushchev's inconsistent behavior when the fleet and aviation were ruined in this country. And how expensive it was to restore these arms. Where does this disrespect towards the opinion of the Army on purely military issues come from? The Army knows better what and how many arms it needs. It's the Army, not the Ministry of Foreign Affairs, that's responsible for the military security of the country. If something happens, we will have to answer for it, not the foreign affairs ministry."

Often, attempts by civilian specialists to look into military problems were sharply rebuffed by the military leadership. Even before the missile issue, the Central Committee Defense Department prepared proposals to have a demilitarized corridor in Central Europe between the military groupings of the Warsaw Pact and NATO to be presented by the Soviet side as the next military-political initiative. The proposals envisaged taking out all NATO and Warsaw Pact nuclear weapons and heavy arms from a three-hundred-kilometer-wide demilitarized zone within two years. These proposals were supported by the Ministry of Foreign Affairs (Vorontsov) and the Central Committee's International Department (Korniyenko).

At a meeting in the Central Committee on this issue, Akhromeyev spoke very sharply and emotionally.

"Are you aware that heavy arms are basically tanks? Do you know how many tanks we would have to pull out of this zone?" the marshal said, beginning to pace the room.

"We know," I said. "Two thousand."

"And do you have any idea where we could store them?"

"We could pull them out into Ukraine, Belorussia, and the Urals and keep them in garages."

"Rubbish! We have no room for our tanks here. They are kept in the open air and get rusty. In Germany, we have well-equipped parking lots. Let them remain there."

Economic reasoning proved to be more convincing than military-political wisdom this time. We failed to reach a consensus.

On a number of issues, Akhromeyev treated me as a channel to the top. He must have thought that he could send signals to the leadership through me, giving to the Central Committee in an informal way opinions and protests of the military against the policy of arms cuts. He was sure that I wouldn't distort or overemphasize what he said, that it would be analyzed and taken into account. He was so sure that his extremely negative statements would not be used against him personally that he could afford to play a very risky game.

Once, before a meeting at Zaikov's on some concrete steps on intermediate- and short-range missile cuts, Akhromeyev said softly to me, "If this really happens I'll hand in my party card."

I understood his personal distress and tried to convince him to take it less emotionally. Akhromeyev offered the greatest resistance to weapons reductions at one of the Politburo meetings. According to the people who were present at that meeting, he didn't find support on the issues concerning stockpiling of weapons and quickly took a different line, emphasizing the danger for the Soviet Union from the American inspection missions which would inevitably accompany the process of cuts and elimination of missiles. Inspections could reveal that the situation in the army wasn't as good as Americans believed it to be. Gorbachev was extremely unhappy and recommended that the chief of staff take better care of the situation in the army, so that he wouldn't need to fear Americans.

"Maybe we'll have to issue special invitations to Americans to get things organized in our army units," said Gorbachev.

At this meeting, Akhromeyev was overpowered. Afterward, he began to take an active part in the process of arms cuts. The change of attitude was very conspicuous, and this depressed him.

Once, when we were waiting for a meeting to begin, he came up to me and said, "I'll retire on the day I'm 65. Not a day more."

I joked that such an active person as he wouldn't be able to stay idle.

Akhromeyev began to participate directly in talks. Quite often, the process required on-the-spot decisions. At these times, the interdepartmental working group remained in the office of the first deputy chief of staff around the clock. Usually, communication between the interdepartmental working group and Soviet delegation was effected by me and Akhromeyev. The problems were discussed on closed channels of communication. If the interdepartmental working group voiced objections, Akhromeyev reacted emotionally. Sometimes, he tried to apply pressure by saying that the issue had already been endorsed by the delegations. Once, I said to him that I was unhappy with such pressure.

"Well, Vitaly Leonidovich," he answered, "I'm unhappy that the local party committees are being destroyed."

When Akhromeyev retired from his position as chief of staff and became Gorbachev's advisor on military-political issues in 1988, he began to do his own analysis of the situation, give advice to, and fulfill direct tasks from, Gorbachev. Because of this, the preparation of some military-political decisions bypassed the interdepartmental working group. As before, Akhromeyev's proposals didn't always prove to be feasible. This was to be expected. One person can't substitute for a think tank, which can do a thorough analysis. Akhromeyev attributed these outcomes to my personal attitude, because I was the main link between him and the interdepartmental working group, through Zaikov's Commission on Talks under the Defense Council (he thought it impossible to communicate through the General Staff of the Armed Forces, which had a new chief, Mikhail Moiseyev).

Akhromeyev voiced his dissatisfaction to Zaikov once when the three of us were in a discussion, saying, "Lev Nikolayevich, it's become very difficult to work with Vitaly Leonidovich. He has become obstinate and puts up obstacles."

I wondered how Zaikov, who was chairman of the Commission on Talks under the Defense Council, would answer. Akhromeyev knew that I was working out points for weapons talks with the help of the chairman of the commission. This meant that he was addressing his concerns to the commission as well.

"That's his job," Zaikov answered. "He is the last block post in our state. If someone made a mistake and he missed it, there would be nobody to stop the process."

This issue was never raised again.

Unlike Akhromeyev, the new chief of staff, Moiseyev, was an ambitious person trying to hold everything in his own hands. At the meetings of the Politburo Military-Industrial Commission, instead of supporting joint efforts to work out a rational decision acceptable to all, he would take one side, which, in a number of cases, resulted in conflict during discussions.

Dmitry Yazov, the new defense minister, by contrast, understood the development of the military-political international situation and the problems of the army and fleet and took a reasonable attitude towards arms and armed-forces cuts. He worked constructively in Zaikov's commission. Once, after a party committee meeting at the General Staff of the Armed Forces, where Communists criticized the military leadership, he did send a letter to the Politburo asking that military problems be taken into account more during talks and that more military specialists work in the delegations. Zaikov's commission looked into the request and didn't object.

Discussions concerning the reductions in the intermediate-range missiles brought about heated debates in the interdepartmental working group and at the Politburo Military-Industrial Commission. Only the Ministry of Foreign Affairs, represented by Karpov and Shevardnadze, stood for Reagan's "zero option"—complete cuts of Soviet and American intermediate-range missiles. The rest were in favor of removing the most dangerous missiles only from Europe but keeping one hundred missiles in the Asian region as a counterbalance to the American bombers based in Japan. Accordingly, the United States could keep one hundred missiles on their territory.

Elimination of almost-new nuclear rockets was an extremely dramatic military-political step for the Soviet Union. It was a kind of sacrilege. This is why complete elimination of the intermediate-range missiles proved to be an insurmountable psychological barrier for the participants in the process. As a result, the Soviet strategy was to conduct the talks on the missile cuts in such a way that both sides would end up with one hundred missiles each. The Ministry of Foreign Affairs failed to break the general resistance to further cuts, and this position was accepted in Reykjavik. But even this decision was a serious victory for the supporters of arms limitation—the radicals.

The American side began to suggest they might modify the Pershing II missiles and deploy them to Alaska, whence they could reach Soviet territory. Such talk, to a certain extent, prompted the rest of the members of both the interdepartmental working group and the Politburo Military-Industrial Commission to change their attitudes, and then the attitude of the Soviet leadership, to favoring a complete elimination of Soviet and American intermediate-range missiles. Besides, the Soviet specialists were piling up arguments in favor of simultaneous cuts of other dangerous arms—operational-tactical missiles which also threatened strategic stability.

A decision was made to completely eliminate intermediate- and short-range missiles. The Ministry of Foreign Affairs promptly prepared concrete proposals for Gorbachev's weapons-reduction initiatives. The Politburo accepted the proposals, and on February 2, 1987, Gorbachev officially proposed the complete elimination of short-range along with intermediate-range missiles to the other side.

In 1988, there was a dramatic outburst of displeasure against the policy of arms reductions from military specialists at one of the party meetings of the legal department of the General Staff of the Armed Forces. The efforts of the Ministry of Foreign Affairs to cut armaments were the target of the attack. The people who took the floor didn't deny, on the whole, the need for a realistic approach to arms limitation, but they objected to large cuts of strategic arms, reductions in nuclear missiles in numbers exceeding the cuts on the American side. The military accused the Ministry of Foreign Affairs of conceding unilaterally to the Americans, of exceeding their powers, and even of spilling some secrets to Americans during the talks. The leadership of the Ministry of Defense and the General Staff of the Armed Forces was accused of taking a pampering attitude and insufficiently resisting the Ministry of Foreign Affairs.

This meeting demonstrated that there was no single attitude towards issues of arms limitation in the military, but there was a growing, silent protest among the military specialists. This protest was not taken into consideration at the interdepartmental working group because the military lacked actual arguments to support their position. However, the meeting did demonstrate that the opposition of the military could significantly hinder the progress of arms limitation. This episode also reaffirmed to me that an independent procedure in the form of the interdepartmental working group for making decisions on military-political problems was set up at the right time, even though it ended the unique right of the military to control this process. If such a body had not been established, the arms limitation problem would have become an ongoing war between the Ministry of Defense and the Ministry of Foreign Affairs or become a unilateral ceding of the most important positions on strategic arms. This second state of affairs was clearly demonstrated at the beginning of the 1990s.

One of the active opponents on a number of arms-reduction proposals was Oleg Baklanov (secretary of the Central Committee, then head of the department on defense and security under the USSR president, and member of the Politburo Military-Industrial Commission). His attitude was that the Soviet and U.S. nuclear arms cuts must be conducted only on the basis of arithmetic equality. I was his deputy in the Defense Department and had to keep him in the know about everything that went on at the talks. I always tried to convince him that the terms of a nuclear confrontation did not necessarily require a strict arithmetic equality, the way this had been necessary in the prenuclear period.

Baklanov sharply criticized the attitude of the Ministry of Foreign Affairs, the work of the delegations, and the work of Zaikov's commission. However, he refrained from making his attitude public. He thought that the president was given one-sided information on arms cuts and was not shown what concessions we had to make during the talks with the American side. He came out with a short article on disarmament topics which was titled something like "There Is No Free Lunch." At the beginning of April 1990, together with the General Staff of the Armed Forces center for operational strategic studies, Baklanov prepared a report for the president on the actual ratio of nuclear weapons the Soviet and Americans had and on the ratio of nuclear weapons the two countries would have in the case of a 50 percent reduction in strategic arms. His report concluded that the talks might lead to the disruption of parity between the superpowers and to unjustified costs. Gorbachev sent this report to Zaikov's commission to be examined. No action was taken on it.

The directors of institutes and defense-industry design bureaus got actively involved in the process of arms cuts. Some directors and specialists from leading institutes and design bureaus took a productive part in the interdepartmental working group and in the Politburo Military-Industrial Commission. They participated in the talks with the American side, gave recommendations on the spot on the texts of documents, and provided scientific and technical support. The directors' corps and defense-industry specialists on the whole accepted the policy of arms limitation and cuts in large part because they had already participated, at a high level, in converting the Soviet defense industry from arms factories to factories making civilian goods. This conversion was scheduled to go on for a long time so as to avoid the tension created by forcing people out of their jobs.

It was not always possible to redirect military facilities to consumer-goods production, however. For example, there was a long dispute over the early-warning-missile-attack-system radar station near Krasnoyarsk. It covered the northeastern missile threat direction. The ABM Treaty of 1972 allowed the construction of such radar stations on the perimeters of the Soviet and U.S. national territories. The Soviet leadership (Brezhnev, Ustinov, and Grechko)—without giving a thought to possible consequences—made a decision to build the station at a place where it was feasible. But this was not at the perimeter. They thought that "perimeter" meant not a formal state border but the line beyond which only a minimal part of the country's population lives. In the Soviet Union, only 5 percent of the population lived to the east of Krasnoyarsk. U.S. plans to build two radar stations outside their own territory (in Greenland and England) also spurred the Soviet leadership. They approved the radar station near Krasnoyarsk in the early 1980s. Later, under Gorbachev, in September 1989, the Soviet Union announced that it would not finish the station. More than 530 million rubles had already been spent and all the infrastructure had been built—a whole town for thirty thousand residents. But the station was an obvious violation of the ABM Treaty. There were attempts to convert it into a scientific center, a plant, a lumber farm, even a correctional facility. Not a single government department wanted to adopt a whole town of thirty thousand people in the depths of the Siberian taiga. The new town was abandoned.

In arms-control delegations, the Central Committee Defense Department representative had an important role. I tried to take advantage of this position as much as possible to push the following approach: to bear in mind that the two sides knew each other very well; not to come out with proposals based on unsubstantiated information; and not to reject all American proposals but to look into them carefully and try to fill them with content advantageous to the Soviet Union. This kind of approach was what was expected—under orders—from a Central Committee representative. Our specialists working in delegations didn't normally try to bluff or come out with proposals unsupported by technical arguments. This sincerity raised the level of mutual trust during weapons-reduction talks and improved the chances of making progress. However, in Geneva, when a Russian delegation of which I was part was working on proposals to be endorsed in Moscow, we had a lot of disagreements. As a result, a representative of the General Staff of the Armed Forces once sent a report to Moscow which claimed that some "conservative" Central Committee representative had blocked a number of solutions.

At the talks, each side had a list of missiles whose range corresponded to the categories of either intermediate-range or short-range. These lists didn't arouse a lot of disputes, with the exception of one Soviet weapon, the SS-23 Oka, which was included on the American list. The issue of the short-range Oka missile was not easily resolved.

The maximum range of the Oka was four hundred kilometers. At that time, it was being modernized to increase the range to six hundred kilometers. The U.S. specialists claimed that the existing range was five hundred kilometers. Our estimates indicated that, technically, their claims could be correct. Had a missile with the Oka's specifications been made using American technology, it would have a longer range. But this missile was not made with American technology; it was a Soviet product. We knew that our estimate of Oka's range—four hundred kilometers—could be proven only by revealing our inadequate rocket technology. Of course, the Oka was omitted from the list made by the Soviet side; no technological characteristics were provided. Americans knew our technological shortcomings. They always included the missile on their lists of weapons which had to be cut.

When delegations met to discuss this point, there was little ground for dispute. During informal breaks, when discussing the missile's range, the Americans used to say that if an American missile with such characteristics could fly five hundred kilometers, sooner or later the Soviet rocket would be able to do it, too. Our argument for omitting the Oka—Soviet technological inferiority—was not good enough to keep it off the negotiating table.

We discussed the Oka among ourselves on several occasions. For example, in October 1987, the following conversation took place at a meeting of the Politburo Military-Industrial Commission, a high-level committee.

Akhromeyev began by saying, "The sides haven't so far announced the minimum range to be eliminated for intermediate- and short-range missiles. The Oka got on the list only as a type of weapon. A political decision was made. There were only two launches at the maximum range of four hundred kilometers. We agreed to eliminate this missile as a goodwill sign."

Karpov responded, "All the same, we're going to put this missile on the list and indicate its range in the memorandum as five hundred kilometers."

"But we tested it for four hundred kilometers," Korniyenko objected.

Then Zaikov took a stand.

"We need to launch it for five hundred kilometers and show its maximum range capacity," he insisted.

Maslyukov worried about setting a disadvantageous precedent by promoting the five-hundred-kilometer range.

"If we accept the estimated range figure, Americans will continue to dictate their technological data to us," he pointed out. "We need to tell them that the decision of the Soviet Union was political and that's why this missile was put on the list."

"Still, we tested the missile for four hundred kilometers, though we included it as a five-hundred-kilometer-range missile. It is a political decision," Zaikov agreed.

"Our way to show the missile's maximum range may come to nothing. If we continue making missiles with Oka characteristics, we'll be violators," Karpov asserted. "They will be included in the five-hundred-kilometer range no matter what."

Then, Shevardnadze said decisively, "We must close this missile line completely."

"According to the Americans' data, Oka's range is 475 kilometers," Aleksandr Bessmertnykh added.

Akhromeyev elaborated on his original position.

"We should specify the range as four hundred kilometers, but the next missile must be made smaller in size," he stated.

"We can't ruin our new developments, but the size of new rockets must be smaller than Oka's," Zaikov concurred.

Akhromeyev spelled out the ramifications of Gorbachev's decision.

"All together, we would have to eliminate 102 launchers, 200 rockets, and 301 warheads of Oka missiles," he said.

"We can remind them that at the beginning of the talks the announced range for negotiation was five hundred to one thousand kilometers. The Americans said they would include missiles with a four-hundred-kilometer range, but we never got around to discussing that. Still, Oka remained on the lists," Korniyenko observed.

"Anyway, we should write four hundred kilometers in the memorandum," Zaikov declared. "We still have another week before the meeting with Shultz in Moscow. We must try to launch the rocket to the distance of 460 kilometers even without targeting. Maslyukov and Oleg Belyakov will organize the work. But it must be the maximum range at launch that counts."

Shortly afterwards, when Gorbachev met George Shultz, then the U.S. secretary of state, in Moscow, the Soviet Union agreed to include Oka in the list of missiles to be eliminated. Akhromeyev was present at the meeting. More than once I tried to get an answer from him about who was there besides him, who had prompted this decision from Gorbachev. According to Akhromeyev, Gorbachev told Shultz about this decision before he arrived in the room, and Akhromeyev couldn't go against a decision already made by the leadership.

The Oka was a major achievement of Segei Nepobedimy's design bureau in Kolomna. Thirty-five Oka rockets were scheduled to be produced and supplied to the army in 1988, but, in December 1987, production of Oka missiles and launchers was stopped completely.

Once, at a banquet, I was sitting next to the chief designer, Nepobedimy. A military man was sitting opposite us. He pointed his finger at me accusingly and said, "This man sold out the Oka." Nepobedimy was holding a fork in his hand at that moment. I looked at the fork with apprehension, wondering what he was going to do with it!

The end of the Oka also aroused a lot of regret in the troops. The rocket had been reliable and easy to maintain. Protest arose in military units against the elimination of the wheeled launchers in particular. There were attempts to keep some segments of the Oka project, at least for "household" needs. This entailed some funny incidents.

About one hundred Oka launchers were to be eliminated in Stankovo (Belorussia). The Intermediate-Range Nuclear Forces Treaty envisaged eleven procedures for disabling them. One was cutting off the back part of the hull of the mobile launcher from the undercarriage. Thirty launchers were eliminated in 1989. However, the technical staff welded the cut-off tail parts back on twenty-four pieces. This made it easier to use the undercarriage for other army needs, and it did not violate the treaty. The strength of the undercarriage was compromised, so it couldn't be used to launch rockets anymore. The American inspectors who were present at the elimination, however, pointed out some "unclear moments" which needed clarifying. The parts that had been welded back on the launchers had to be cut off again. The defense minister issued a disciplinary reprimand.

A future for Oka missiles was also found in Czechoslovakia, the German Democratic Republic, and Bulgaria. Between 1985 and 1987, sixteen launchers, seventy-two missiles, and forty-nine cluster non-nuclear warheads were delivered to these Warsaw Pact countries. The Soviet Union decided that these missiles could remain in these countries for the term of their technical life and that the Warsaw Pact countries could run them on their own. However, it was said that the Soviet leadership would understand if they proposed eliminating Oka earlier.

At the Politburo Military-Industrial Commission, Akhromeyev took upon himself the preparation for withdrawing the Oka missile from the Warsaw Pact countries. The specialists of the interdepartmental working group took this move calmly. Why did they not object to the loss of these excellent missiles, costing 344,000 rubles (approximately $240,000) each? Didn't the Soviet Union need that missile

and similar intermediate- and short-range missiles for the security
of the country?

The specialists of the nonmilitary section of the interdepartmental working group thought that, for all the surrounding countries,
short-range ground-based nuclear weapons were the most "incon-
venient" and dangerous ones in the deterrence arsenals. They are
particularly dangerous in densely populated Europe. A number
of institutes studied the results of a nuclear attack on the Soviet
Union. These studies showed that fifty nuclear blasts in Europe would
turn its territory into a Chernobyl in terms of contamination. The
Chernobyl catastrophe made it possible to overturn the euphoric
assumptions of nuclear strategists, which had been based on the
explosions in Hiroshima and Nagasaki.

Short-range missiles were meant to hit deep into the attacking
enemy's territory. This is why they were deployed relatively close
to the border—less than one hundred kilometers. The West's technology—for example, tanks with gas-turbine engines—made it possible to reach the place of an opponent's missile launch in forty
to fifty minutes. A missile launcher can move at a speed of forty
kilometers per hour, so a potential enemy's tank could quickly get
close enough to shoot at it using high-precision weapons.

What choice could one make with these technologies at hand?
In this case, this determination was entrusted to the commander of
the battleground. His options weren't great, though: he could either
launch his country's nuclear missile quickly onto the territory of an
enemy who had sent a tank, thus starting a nuclear war; or he could
destroy his country's missile installation together with the nuclear
missile, thus dispersing the nuclear charge onto his own territory;
or, he could surrender his country's missile, with all the destructive
power it possesses, to the enemy. Which of these was better?

The main question concerning the use of nuclear weapons is the
expediency of such a catastrophic step. Any nuclear attack may
result in retaliation. Nobody can foresee how far an exchange of the
nuclear strikes will go after the first nuclear explosion. The Soviet
Union could retaliate with a strategic nuclear-missile attack on

U.S. territory if the United States sent a short-range nuclear missile against the Soviet troops on the European front. Is it a good thing to do, to resolve a battlefield problem by triggering a suicidal nuclear disaster? Our specialists took into account the consequences of an enemy battlefield combat operation (for example, occupying a border town) and the unpredictable consequences of nuclear retaliation. They came to the conclusion that most likely a nuclear attack with a short-range missile will never take place. A less serious approach to short-range weapons, as if they were only slightly nuclear, is not justified. What makes them most dangerous is their close proximity to the chaos of a battlefield. This lowers the nuclear threshold and poses a threat in the form of terrorism.

The Soviet specialists came to the conclusion that short-range nuclear missiles in Europe, like intermediate-range missiles, pose a mutual threat and must be the first to be eliminated. For this reason, the Soviet Union came out with proposals to eliminate them together with intermediate-range missiles. American and West German Pershing I missiles were also eliminated. When these proposals were carried out, nuclear security in the world increased considerably.

I believe Gorbachev made a correct decision concerning Oka. He enhanced the security of the Soviet Union and the world. For this reason, the specialists of the interdepartmental working group had nothing against it. Unfortunately, attempts to build new tactical nuclear weapons are still going on. Those who are trying to revive this type of weapons should remember the old saying—it is the fire that has already died out that may cause the biggest flames.

Afterword

In addition to snapshots from a career in rocket design and the insider's view of arms development and limitation, he shares in this book, Vitaly Katayev also compiled, as part of his memoir, a list of treaty texts he wrote while in the interdepartmental working group and a list of personal initiatives he undertook to work out objective solutions on military-political, military-technical, and other issues related to the country's security. These lists are presented below.

Topics of Treaties

- elimination of short- and intermediate-range missiles (ratified in 1988)
- limitation and reduction of strategic arms (ratified 11.04.92)
- conventional weapons in Europe (ratified 07.08.92)
- space weapons
- disposal and nonproduction of chemical weapons and measures to promote multilateral convention on banning chemical weapons (signed 06.01.90)
- control over observing the 1972 convention on banning biological weapons
- limitation of underground weapons tests (treaties went into force in 12.11.90)
- nonproliferation of missiles and missile technology (signed in June 1990)

- introducing regimes of "open sky" and "open land," etc. (signed 03.04.92)
- prevention of dangerous military activity (signed 06.12.89)

Personal Initiatives

- elimination of short- and intermediate-range missiles, including demonstration to foreign specialist of such elimination on August 28, 1988
- measures to reach the world standards of weight/size capacity of warheads of Soviet missiles
- joint experiment on control over nuclear weapons in Semipalatinsk Test Site and the Nevada test site
- establishment of national centers to reduce nuclear threat (Sam Nunn and John W. Warner expressed the same idea)
- demonstration to Organization for Security and Cooperation in Europe of modern Soviet hardware
- experiment on the Black Sea to check presence of nuclear weapons on board a ship
- establishment of an International Agency of Space Observation (not accepted because of organizational and legal difficulties)
- use of heavy missiles to render assistance to those in distress (got a patent)
- establishment of a demilitarized zone 300 km between Warsaw Pact countries and NATO (development of Olof Palme's idea). General Staff of the Armed Forces and Ministry of Defense went only as far as establishing a nuclear free corridor.
- Council of Ministers resolution on Ust-Katav development
- reconstruction of the Tchaikovsky museum
- construction of sports centers and creativity centers for children in Zlatoust

Appendix A
Alternative Names for
Soviet Rockets and Missiles

Vitaly Katayev uses multiple nomenclatures to refer to rockets and missiles. The following list, organized by type, tracks alternative names for the rockets and missiles he refers to, arranged in alphabetical and numerical order. Each entry begins with the Soviet military name and any code name. The Ministry of Defense's GRAU index or a Soviet industry number follows, where applicable, after a colon. The NATO reporting name appears at the end of relevant entries.

Short-Range Ballistic Missiles

R-400 Oka: GRAU 9K714; NATO SS-23 Spider

Intermediate-Range Ballistic Missiles

R-12/R-12 Dvina (silo-launched): GRAU 8K63; NATO SS-4 Sandal
R-14 Chusovaya: GRAU 8K65; NATO SS-5 Skean

Submarine-Launched Ballistic Missiles

D-2: launch system for R-13
D-11: launch system for R-31
D-19: launch system for R-39
R-13: 4K50; NATO SS-N-4 Sark
R-29R Volna: 3M40; NATO SS-N-18 Stingray
R-29RM Shtil: NATO SS-N-23 Skiff

R-31: 3M17; NATO SS-N-17 Snipe

R-39 Rif: GRAU 3M64, 3M20, and 3R65; NATO SS-N-20 Sturgeon

Intercontinental Ballistic Missiles

R-7 Semyorka: GRAU 8K71; NATO SS-6 Sapwood

R-9/R-9A Desna: NATO SS-8 Sasin

R-16: GRAU 8K64; NATO SS-7 Saddler

R-26: GRAU 8K66

R-36: GRAU 8K67; NATO SS-9 Scarp

R-36M: GRAU 15A14, 15A18; NATO SS-18 Satan

RT-1: 8K95

RT-21 Temp-2S: 15Zh42; NATO SS-16 Sinner

RT-23 Molodets: GRAU 15Zh44; NATO SS-24 Scalpel

UR-100MR Sotka: 15A15; NATO SS-17 Spanker

UR-100N: 15A30; NATO SS-19 Stiletto

Other Spacecraft

Kosmos: GRAU 11K63

N-1

RK-100/R-56: 8K68

Appendix B
Scientific, Political, and Military Figures in Vitaly Katayev's Account of the Soviet Missile Age

Vitaly Katayev mentions many scientific, political, and military figures active in the Soviet missile age. This list specifies their roles during the period he describes.

Afanasyev, Sergei. Minister of general machine-building, 1965–1983

Akhromeyev, Sergei. Senior representative of the Ministry of Defense and the General Staff of the Armed Forces in the interdepartmental working group

Alekseyev, Nikolai. Deputy defense minister, 1970–1980

Allé, Yuri. Head of the serial-production design department at Omsk Civil Aviation Plant

Andropov, Yuri. General Secretary of the Central Committee, 1982–1984

Avtonomov, Valentin. Member of the initial team of project designers on the R-16

Baklanov, Oleg. Member of the Politburo Military-Industrial Commission; secretary of the Central Committee on defense issues, 1988–1991; head of the department on defense and security under the USSR president

Barmin, Vladimir. Designer of rocket launch complexes

Belousov, Igor. Minister of shipbuilding industry; deputy chairman of the Council of Ministers; chairman of the Military-Industrial Commission of the Council of Ministers, 1988–1990

Belyakov, Oleg. Head of the Central Committee Defense Department, 1985–1991

Bessmertnykh, Aleksandr. Deputy foreign minister, 1986–1990

Bondarenko, Anton. R-16 test operator

Bratsky, Sasha. Test operator at Baikonur

Brezhnev, Leonid. General Secretary of the Central Committee, 1964–1982

Budnik, Vasily. First chief deputy at Yuzhnoye Design Bureau; test manager on R-16

Butoma, Boris. Worked on R-16 with rocket gyroscopes

Chebrikov, Viktor. Head of the KGB, 1982–1988

Chelomei, Vladmir. Chief designer of rocket design bureau OKB 52, 1955–1984

Chernenko, Konstantin. General Secretary of the Central Committee, 1984–1985

Chervov, Nikolai. Represented the General Staff of the Armed Forces in the interdepartmental working group

Dementyev, Pyotr. Minister of Aviation Industry, 1953–1965 and 1967–1977

Derkach, Valentin. Engines test operator on R-16 in Baikonur

Detinov, Nikolai. Represented the Military-Industrial Commission of the Council of Ministers in the interdepartmental working group

Dmitriyev, Igor. Head of Central Committee Defense Department, 1965–1981

Dobrynin, Anatoly. Ambassador of the Soviet Union in the USA, 1962–1986; Secretary of the Central Committee, 1986–1988

Frunze, Mikhail. Namesake of Arsenal Design Bureau and a Bolshevik leader of the Russian Revolution of 1917

Galas, Mikhail. Leading designer of 8K66 and R-14

Gerchik, Konstantin. Chief of Launch Complexes at Baikonur test range, 1958–1961

Glushko, Valentin. Major chief designer of the rocket and space age, head of rocket design bureaus, 1944–1989

Golovko, Konstantin. Director of Omsk Aviation Plant

Grachyov, Viktor. Technical director of tests in Baikonur; deputy for tests at Yuzhnoye Design Bureau

Grechko, Andrei. Minister of Defense, 1967–1976

Grigoryev, Yuri. Deputy for projects planning at Makeyev's design bureau; worked at the Central Committee defense department

Grishin, Lev. Deputy chairman of the State Committee of the Council of Ministers for Defense Technology, 1958–1960

Gromyko, Andrei. Minister of Foreign Affairs, 1957–1985

Gubanov, Boris. First deputy on the SS-17 at Yuzhnoye Design Bureau

Gusev, Andrei. Administrative head of the expedition in Baikonur

Ishlinsky, Aleksandr. Pioneering academician in cosmonautics; director of Institute for Problems in Mechanics, 1965–1990

Kaibyshev, Oskar. Metallurgist and deputy of the Supreme Soviet

Kalashnikov, Aleksei. Head of the division at the Rocket Armaments Main Department

Kalmykov, Valery. Soviet minister in charge of radioelectronics; worked on R-16

Karpov, Viktor. Represented the Ministry of Foreign Affairs in the interdepartmental working group

Kashanov, Erik. Head of design work on the R-36 at Yuzhnoye Design Bureau

Keldysh, Mstislav. Scientist in the field of mathematics and mechanics; president of the Academy of Sciences, 1961–1975

Khrushchev, Sergei. Son of General Secretary Nikita Khrushchev; participated in development of missile technology at Chelomei's design bureau

Kolupayev, Yakov. Director of Omsk Civil Aviation Plant

Korniyenko, Georgy. Represented the International Department of the Central Committee in the interdepartmental working group

Korolyov, Sergei. Founder, chief designer, and namesake of pioneering rocket design bureau OKB 1, 1946–1966

Kovalchuk, Valentin. Head of group working on RK-100 at Yuzhnoye Design Bureau

Kovalyov, Sergei. Designer of submarines for carrying missiles at Rubin Central Design Bureau for Marine Engineering

Kovtunenko, Vladimir. Head of planning office and head of space division at Yuzhnoye Design Bureau

Kozlov, Frol. Second secretary of the Central Committee, 1960–1963

Kozlov, Mikhail. Head of the Main Operations Directorate of the
General Staff of the Armed Forces

Krasavtsev, Vyacheslav. Supervisor of the Buran project

Krasnov, Evgeny. Defense Department instructor from defense plant
in Kovrov

Krylov, Nikolai. Commander-in-chief of the Strategic Rocket Forces,
1963–1972

Kryuchkov, Vladimir. Represented the KGB in the interdepartmental
working group

Kuchma, Leonid. Leading designer for space systems and technical
manager at Baikonur; general director of Yuzhmash, 1986–1992;
prime minister of Ukraine, 1992–1993; president of Ukraine,
1994–2005

Kukushkin, Vladimir. Head of sector in pneumatic hydro systems of
engine systems at Yuzhnoye Design Bureau

Kurushin, Aleksandr. Chief of launching pad No. 43 in Baikonur

Kuznetsov, Nikolai. Chief designer of aircraft-engine design bureau
OKB 276, 1949–1994

Leonov, Nikolai. Represented KGB in the interdepartmental working
group

Ligachev, Yegor. A leading Soviet politician in Central Committee

Luarsabov, Kostya. Engine expert for the R-16 in Nedelin disaster

Makeyev, Viktor Petrovich. Chief designer at rocket design bureau
SKB 385, 1955–1985

Maslyukov, Yuri. Chairman of the Military-Industrial Commission of
the Council of Ministers, 1985–1988, 1991

Matrenin, Aleksandr, Head of the assembly-testing facility in Baikonur

Moiseyev, Mikhail. Chief of the Soviet General Staff of the Armed
Forces, 1988–1991

Moskalenko, Kirill. Commander-in-chief of Strategic Rocket Forces,
1960–1962; chief inspector of the Ministry of Defense

Mozzhorin, Yuri. Director of space-program research bureau NII 88,
1961–1990

Mrykin, Aleksandr. Head of the Main Directorate for Missile Weapons

Nazarenko, Arnold. Worked on the initial team of project designers
for R-16

Nedelin, Mitrofan. Chief marshal of artillery; deputy minister of defense, 1955–1960; commander-in-chief of Strategic Rocket Forces, 1959–1960

Nepoklonov, Boris. Head of group at Omsk Civil Aviation Plant

Petrov, Boris. Soviet scientist in mechanics and mathematics; chairman of the Interkosmos Council

Petrov, Gerold. Top student at Kazan Aviation Institute and family friend

Pilyugin, Nikolai. Designer specializing in control systems for rocket boosters and spacecraft

Polysayev, Aleksei. Leading designer of the R-16 missile complex

Radutny, Viktor. Deputy chief designer for engines in Baikonur

Romanov, Grigory. Central Committee secretary and Politburo member responsible for defense industry, 1983–1985

Rudnev, Konstantin. Deputy minister of defense industry, 1953–1958; chairman of State Committee of Council of Ministers for Defense Technology, 1958–1961

Rudyak, Yevgeny. Designer of artillery and missile systems, worked on R-16

Ryabikov, Vasily. Chairman of Military-Industrial Commission of the Council of Ministers, 1955–1957; member of Sputnik State Commission and Politburo Commission on Rocket Equipment

Semyonov, Anatoly. Head of the Rocket Armaments Main Department

Serbin, Ivan. Head of Central Committee defense-industry department, 1958–1981

Sergeyev, Vladimir. Chief designer of spacecraft-control-system design bureau OKB 692, 1960–1986

Shakirov, Midkhat. First secretary of the Bashkortostan oblast committee

Shevardnadze, Eduard. Minister of Foreign Affairs, 1985–1990

Smirnov, Leonid. Director of Yuzhny Machine-Building Plant, 1952–1961; chairman of State Committee of the Council of Ministers for Defense Technology, 1961–1963; chairman of the Military-Industrial Commission of the Council of Ministers, 1963–1985

Sokolov, Sergei. Minister of Defense, 1984–1987

Spassky, Igor. Designer of submarines for carrying missiles at Rubin Central Design Bureau for Marine Engineering

Starodubov, Viktor. Represented the International Department of the Central Committee in the interdepartmental working group

Stroganov, Boris. Head of sector at Yuzhnoye Design Bureau; head of general machine-building sector at Central Committee Defense Department, 1965–1987

Tupolev, Andrei. Pioneering Soviet aircraft designer; namesake of design bureau and many aircraft

Tyulin, Georgy. First deputy minister of General Machine-Building, 1965–1976

Us, Stanislav. Leading designer for the R-36

Ustinov, Dmitry. Chairman of the Military-Industrial Commission of the Council of Ministers, 1957–1963; Central Committee secretary, 1965–1976; Minister of Defense of the Soviet Union, 1976–1984

Utkin, Vladimir. Early designer at Yuzhnoye Design Bureau, became chief designer (later called general designer), 1971–1991

Varennikov, Valentin. Deputy head of the General Staff of the Armed Forces, 1979–1989

Varyvdin, Vadim. Worked at Yuzhnoye Design Bureau in antennae

Vorontsov, Yuli. Represented the Ministry of Foreign Affairs in the interdepartmental working group

Voroshilov, Kliment. Chairman of the Supreme Soviet Presidium, 1953–1960

Yangel, Mikhail. Chief designer of Yuzhnoye Design Bureau, 1954–1971

Yazov, Dmitry. Minister of Defense, 1987–1991

Yelenevich, Boris. Director of Omsk Civil Aviation Plant

Yepishev, Aleksei. Chief of the Main Political Directorate of the Soviet Army and Navy, 1962–1985

Zaikov, Lev. Secretary of Central Committee and head of the defense industry, 1985–1990, serving as chairman of the Commission on Talks under the Defense Council

Notes

PREFACE

1. Throughout this book, rockets and missiles will primarily be identified by their Soviet designations. Please see Appendix A for equivalent NATO reporting names and GRAU indices.

2. "Instructor" is a specific Soviet position which implied monitoring of work within the regional bodies and enterprises for a certain scope of activity (defense, heavy industry, etc.).

3. "Academician" in this context is a professional distinction which means that the person was a full member of the Academy of Sciences of the USSR.

INTRODUCTION

1. John G. Hines, Ellis M. Mishulovich, and John F. Shull, Soviet Intentions, 1965–1985. Volume 1: "An Analytical Comparison of U.S. Soviet Assessments during the Cold War," BDM Federal Inc., Sept. 22, 1995, commissioned by the Office of Net Assessment, Office of the Secretary of Defense, Department of Defense.

Part I

CHAPTER 1

1. Under the system in place at the time, Soviet graduates of such institutes were essentially assigned where to work by special placing commissions.

2. Gorky is a big city on the Volga river, now named Nizhny Novgorod.

3. A five mark is equal to an A grade.

4. *Znaniye* means "knowledge."

5. In the Soviet educational system, a student would get a "diploma of specialist" when she or he passed all the final university exams. A "young specialist," therefore, was a person who had just graduated from a university and was beginning his or her career.

6. The *Sovnarkhoz* was a regional economic council.

7. A cardan joint is a mechanism in a rigid rod that allows the rod to bend in any direction and is commonly used in shafts that transmit rotary motion. It consists of a pair of hinges located close together, oriented at 90° to each other, connected by a cross-shaft.

8. Vnukovo airport is near Moscow.

9. A *bayan* is an accordion with broad reeds.

10. DOSAAF is the Volunteer Society of Assistance to the Army, Aviation, and Fleet.

11. The speaker refers to the Dnieper River, after which the city of Dnepropetrovsk is named.

12. The official exchange rate in 1960 was four rubles to the dollar. One thousand rubles would be approximately equivalent to $250. This would be a good monthly salary in the USSR since prices for food and utilities were not high.

CHAPTER 2

1. This song is an Italian romance ("Dicitencello Vuie") that was very popular at that time.

2. The design bureau was within the plant. At this time, the plant had no name other than the number 586. It was renamed Southern Mechanical Engineering Plant (Yuzhnyi Mashinostroitelnyi Zavod) in 1965, which included the design bureau known as Yuzhnoye and the factory known as Yuzhmash. Yuzhnoye and Yuzhmash are used throughout this book to refer to the design bureau and factory, respectively, even before the official name change.

3. Zhukovsky is a city in the Moscow region, which is known for its designing and testing facilities and scientific-research institutes for aircraft and spacecraft.

CHAPTER 4

1. When the rank of "leading designer of a missile complex" was changed to "chief designer of a missile complex," the existing title "chief designer," which had designated the very top design position at a design bureau, became "general designer." For the sake of consistency with

the earlier period, the older titles will be used throughout this book, with "chief designer" referring to the chief designer of an entire design bureau, unless otherwise specified.

2. The Volga was a prestigious official Soviet car.

CHAPTER 5

1. The Gold Star medal is a special insignia that identifies recipients of the title Hero of the Soviet Union.

2. Dmitry Ustinov.

CHAPTER 6

1. This pioneers' camp was for members of the Young Pioneer Organization of the Soviet Union, which is comparable to the American boy- and girl-scout youth organizations.

Part II

CHAPTER 8

1. Staraya Ploschad is a street in Moscow.

Vitaly Katayev at a competition with a glider that he made himself, ca. 1950.

Katayev (*right*) and his friend Vadim Varyvdin (*left*) playing accordion in the jazz band at boys' school number 9 in Perm, 1950.

Katayev in his army
uniform, early 1950s.

Katayev playing piano (*opposite page*), guitar, and balalaika, 1950s.

Katayev at Omsk Civil Aviation Plant, where he worked from 1956 to 1960.

Katayev hiking, late 1950s.

Katayev on vacation in the Caucasus Mountains, 1958.

Katayev at a friend's place, 1958.

Vitaly and Galina
Katayev, newly
wed, 1958.

Vitaly and Galina Katayev by the Dnieper River at sunset, 1965.

Katayev with his daughter Marina at the annual November 7th celebration of the Great October Socialist Revolution, 1965.

Left to right: Vitaly, Galina, and Marina Katayev with Vitaly's mother,
Nadezhda, on vacation in Yevpatoria, 1967.

Vitaly and Galina
Katayev on vacation
in the Carpathian
Mountains, 1969.

May 1st International Labor Day celebration, early 1970s.

Vitaly Katayev on vacation, 1973.

Katayev in a newly acquired family car, 1975.

Katayev shooting a photograph, 1976. Developing film at home was one of his hobbies.

Vitaly and Galina Katayev with Vitaly's sister Emilia (*center*), on vacation in Yalta, 1977.

Katayev with granddaughter Ksenia, 1987.

Katayev while on
a business trip to
India, late 1980s.

Katayev in Washington, D.C., early 1990s.

Katayev while at an academic conference in London, late 1990s.

Vitaly and Galina Katayev at home in Moscow, early 2000s.

About the Author

Born in 1932, Vitaly Leonidovich Katayev was still actively research-ing and teaching aviation and rocket engineering when he died in 2001. A venerable academician, he had been a senior research scientist since 1997 in the Stability and Nonlinear Dynamics Research Center of the Institute of Machine Science of the Russian Academy of Sciences. From 1992 to 2000 he had also been applying his knowledge as a former government insider in the role of director general of the Military-Industrial-Complex Business Centre. This followed a brief stint in 1992 as first deputy head of the State Counsellor Service for Defence Industry Conversion in the administration of the first Russian Federation president, Boris Yeltsin. Katayev had also served under the last Soviet head of state, Mikhail Gorbachev, as deputy head of the National Defence and Security Department. Prior to the disintegration of the USSR, Katayev spent some sixteen years working in the Defence Department of the Central Committee of the Communist Party. Rising to the post of deputy department chief, he organized an interdepartmental working group of key experts on arms limitation known as "the five," which also worked within the Politburo Defence Council commission. He personally participated in international arms-limitation talks and drafted many treaty texts. After graduating in 1956 from Kazan Aviation Institute, Katayev started his career as an engineer, first at the Omsk Civil Aviation Plant and later at Yuzhnoye Design Bureau and the test range known as Baikonur, the world's first and largest space-launch facility. He was leading designer of strategic missile systems including the R-16 (SS-7 Saddler) and R-36 (SS-9 Scarp), SS-17 Spanker, as well as the Interkosmos space system launched by the missile R-12 (SS-4 Sandal) and DS satellites.

Index